HAGS AND HEROES

Marie-Louise von Franz, Honorary Patron

**Studies in Jungian Psychology
by Jungian Analysts**

Daryl Sharp, General Editor

HAGS AND HEROES

A Feminist Approach
to
Jungian Psychotherapy with Couples

POLLY YOUNG-EISENDRATH

Canadian Cataloguing in Publication Data

Young-Eisendrath, Polly, 1947-
   Hags and heroes

(Studies in Jungian psychology by Jungian analysts; 18)

Bibliography: p.
Includes index.

ISBN 0-919123-17-1

1. Marital psychotherapy. 2. Intimacy (Psychology).
3. Femininity (Psychology). 4. Jung, C.G. (Carl
Gustav), 1875-1961. I. Title. II. Series.

RC488.5.Y68 1984   616.89'15   C84-099207-6

INNER CITY BOOKS
Box 1271, Station Q, Toronto, Canada M4T 2P4
Telephone (416) 927-0355

Honorary Patron: Marie-Louise von Franz.
Publisher and General Editor: Daryl Sharp.
Editorial Board: Fraser Boa, Daryl Sharp, Marion Woodman.

INNER CITY BOOKS was founded in 1980 to promote the
understanding and practical application of the work of C.G. Jung.

Cover: Pen and ink drawing by Canadian artist Anne B. Knoop.
   (Publisher's Collection)

Index by Daryl Sharp.

Printed and bound in Canada by Webcom Limited

Contents

See last pages for descriptions of other INNER CITY BOOKS

1

The Use of Stories in Psychotherapy

When I speak of one's finally being free to devote one's abilities to . . . whatever . . . you wish to quote as durable justification for life . . . that comes only when one has established a relationship of love in both the biologically and culturally ordained . . . sense.
—Harry Stack Sullivan[1]

A story provides the context for this book, a story about power and weakness, about heroics and conflict. It is a story from the famous Knights of the Round Table, but it does not concern battle, dragons or war. It is the story of Sir Gawain and the Lady Ragnell. Although it involves challenge and confrontation, it does not include destruction or conquest. It is an heroic adventure, but one of a kind that would have been more familiar to people in the Middle Ages in Europe than it is to us. It is a medieval romance, an account of the fears and perils in the adventure of embracing human relationship, especially relationship between the sexes. Cherishing another's autonomy as if it were one's own, and caring for another's needs in the same way, are the tasks that we will encounter.

Our story depicts a special problem in human living, the problem of basic trust in intimate, male-female adult relationship. The story accomplishes its goal of instruction by entertaining us, as it did its fifteenth-century audiences, with humor and elegance of image.

As a Jungian psychotherapist, I have come to use stories in ways remarkably similar to ways in which stories have been used by people of all strata of life, in both primitive and sophisticated cultures, for thousands of years. I use stories to guide me in understanding what I cannot grasp with reason. When I listen to the individual story of a person's life, presented as a narrative in psychotherapy or psychoanalysis, I seek to place it in the context of other universal stories I have come to love. Legends, folktales and fairytales were traditionally used to instruct people in ways essential to the smooth functioning of life in human groups. My use of stories is entirely congruent with this purpose.

As maps of the typical configurations of human life in the social group, stories provide guidance to help us find our way through the crises and transitions of the human life cycle: birth, infant bonding, initiation from youth to adulthood, adult bonding and transcending personal loss in aging—all critical periods in personal development. Personality disintegration and reintegration occur with these life transitions. Personal meaning, empathy and motivation must be entirely reworked at each major stage of life in order for a person to continue developing. The major tasks entailed in "paradigm shift," to use the terminology of T. S. Kuhn concerning the structure of scientific revolutions of thought, have been traditionally recognized as perilous.[2] Individuals must depend on each other and the context of the social group to make life transitions safely and meaningfully. Traditional stories are the maps and records we have from other periods and societies to assist us in navigating critical life transitions. It is only in our modern period that we have become blind to our need for the common sense instruction we get from stories.

The story of Sir Gawain and the Lady Ràgnell, recorded in several forms in fifteenth- and sixteenth-century English literature, is a story my co-therapist and I use to assess and treat couples whose relationships have broken down in the area of basic trust or attachment. Breakdown typically takes place in middle life, roughly after the age of thirty-five, or in a comparable phase. The characteristics of crisis in intimate adult attachment include despair, defeat, resentment, boredom and bitterness (a cold and enduring hurt) as regular experiences in the couple's everyday life. Each partner describes a feeling of alienation within the relationship: each person feels bound in a relationship which no longer seems to promise satisfaction, but which seems to demand duty and service. Both partners have been attempting to cope with their dissatisfactions through some version of "living out in the woods" or being only marginally involved with each other. For example, the woman may not be speaking to her husband or children, while the man may be seeing another woman or women "on the side" and feeling removed from his roles of partner and father in the family. Both people just naturally live in a conflict-habituated style of relationship in which they assume that their marriage vows bind them to each other contrary to their own desires to separate.

The story of Sir Gawain and the Lady Ragnell provides a unique map or template through which to view a woman's response to loss of basic trust. Basic trust is defined as both a sense of "continuity of being" (to use D. W. Winnicott's term) in relationship and as the experience of secure reliance on another person to provide for one's primary emotional needs within the interpersonal field of that relationship.[3] Basic trust is synonymous here with attachment and specifically related to John Bowlby's concepts of attachment and loss in human relationship.[4]

The attachment of infant to parent is the initial interpersonal field in which the archetypes of Great Mother and Terrible Mother, as typical human experiences, are activated. In the next chapter I will explain in detail my use of the Jungian concepts of archetype and complex; for our purposes here in considering basic trust, we need only the images of Great and Terrible Mother, of the provident goddess and the dreaded hag, to help us grasp the characteristics of attachment that we will explore. More specifically, when a woman feels continuous and "held," or adequately embraced, in a relationship of basic trust with a man, she experiences herself as an agentive "person." As members of our species, we are "personal" when we feel ourselves to be agents of our own lives (or "useful" to others) and to be worthwhile or esteemed. We feel ourselves to be contributing members of our species, reflected by our partners as adequate, agentive and valued.

The image of Great Mother, as authority and nurturer, is the positive emotional experience of knowing one's love is "good." Interpersonally, it is the experience of being loved, held and nurtured by the other, of feeling oneself as good. We all need Great Mother experiences to feel that our nurturance is bountiful and powerfully good. The image of Terrible Mother, as savage goddess or hag, is the negative and overwhelming emotional experience of knowing one's love is "bad" and feeling oneself as ugly, mean, overwhelming and destructive. Both negative and positive attachment experiences involve strength and power; both are necessary in relationship, but neither should become the dominant mode for personal identity on a continuing basis. As with other archetypal states, Great Mother and Terrible Mother are transitory identity experiences which are "bigger" than a person.

The story of Sir Gawain and the Lady Ragnell sketches out in a clear and practical way the problem of identifying with the hag or Terrible Mother. The hag, nag or bitch of contemporary couple relationships is quite prominent in psychotherapy literature as the domineering, suffocating and overwhelming mother who must control family life at everyone's expense. Through the help of the story, we come to respect the hag and to see her dilemma empathically. We learn that when relationships reach a breakdown in basic trust, when all rational solutions have failed and both partners are alienated, we should listen to the hag. Only she knows the answer that will restore trust to the relationship.

Our story is a gift that cannot be rationally explained. Those who have grown up reading stories for only private pleasure will wonder how this story can be applied so seriously to couple relationships and how it can work to explain so much that is contemporary when it originated at least 500 years ago. It is possible that the contract of marriage, which was established in its present form in the Middle Ages, ties us back to a time so long ago. It is also possible that the story simply makes sense on such a fundamental human level that it transcends the hundreds of years of culture between its time and our own. As a gift, this story provides an extraordinary lens for understanding what Jungians refer to as "devaluing of the feminine."

Before we turn to Sir Gawain and the Lady Ragnell, I will present certain Jungian and feminist concepts that will provide the necessary framework for my reading and interpretation of the story.

The Importance of the Archetypal Feminine

For our purposes here, the *archetypal feminine* is the province of relating and care-giving. This is the domain of sustaining human and natural life within the human group. In other words, it concerns joining, attachment and involvement with people, things and ideas. Its opposite, the *archetypal masculine,* is the domain of distancing and separating. The masculine is characterized here as binding off, separating from, and aggression toward nature and human beings for survival purposes. The masculine involves dividing and separating, waging war and making boundaries, as well as analyzing people, things and ideas as opposed to the experience of joining with them. The following statement from Peggy Sanday, an anthropologist who has studied gender-related power differences in over 150 tribal and modern societies, further clarifies these distinctions as they pertain to human relating and culture:

> One is struck with the degree to which the sexes conform to a rather basic conceptual symmetry, which is grounded in primary sex differences. Women give birth and grow children; men kill and make weapons. Men display their kills (be it an animal, a human head, or a scalp) with the same pride that women hold up the newly born. If birth and death are among the necessities of existence, then men and women contribute equally but in quite different ways to the continuance of life, and hence of culture.[5]

Because there are serious anthropological questions about whether these archetypal themes of "primary sex differences" are actually universally sorted out along the same gender lines (i.e., feminine for women and masculine for men), I do not assume that women and men represent these archetypal domains through their gender identities. Rather, I have come to see both domains as potentially available to each gender for both identity and action purposes.

Our story helps us to understand what happens in intimate relations when the ordinary tasks of care-giving—managing a household, rearing children, sustaining emotional contact and soothing and healing wounds—are devalued. When women and men devalue these activities, whether consciously or unconsciously, they fall into those habitual patterns and modes of relating which are connoted by the Jungian idea of the *negative mother complex*. This complex comprises behaviors, ideas, images and feelings that are concerned with escaping the intimacy of giving and receiving care. The negative mother complex is thus related to the idea of devaluing or excising the feminine from one's identity and activity.

In our present society, men have a tendency to devalue the feminine in themselves and in women. Many feminine attributes are considered "weakness" in traditional male gender identity. Consequently, men struggle to exclude and differ with women and with the concerns of care-giving in order to maintain separate identities as males. Sociologist Nancy Chodorow traces this devaluing of the feminine to exclusively female mothering of the young in our culture:

> Women's universal mothering role has effects both on the development of masculine and feminine personality and on the relative status of the sexes. . . . As long as women must live through their children, and men do not genuinely contribute to socialization and provide easily accessible role models, women will continue to bring up sons whose identity depends on devaluing femininity inside and outside themselves.[6]

Since women are the primary care-takers during almost everyone's childhood years, the voice of female authority rings powerful tones. Men do not simply differ with women rationally or objectively; rather, they often feel what Karen Horney has called "dread of women" and feel compelled to fight the feminine (both inside and outside) in order to experience any personal power in their male identity.

Women, on the other hand, must identify both with the devalued, "inferior" aspects of the feminine and with the powerful projections of female authority. Women feel at once too weak and too powerful in their mothering and authority. When basic trust is low and devaluing the feminine is high, then a woman tends to feel quite wholly identified with the negative and inferior powers of the hag, the witch or the Terrible Mother.

Masculine gender identity in our society tends to rest on the qualities of distancing: men seek to be rational, independent, objective and principled. Often when we women are critical of men, we characterize them as being too remote; we see them as cold, detached, unfeeling and severe. Men's work is generally removed; it is away from home and family, and often away from women and from the emotional world of feeling involvements. Men are rarely called too nurturant, overly yielding or too enveloping. Words that connote female care-giving and mothering are rarely attached to men's identity, even when we are being critical of them.

Men must exclude the feminine from their identity far more vigilantly and strenuously than women have to exclude the masculine. In fact, women can and readily do identify with all aspects of being masculine—from appearance, such as wearing pants and ties, to roles, such as fathering their children and being executive leaders. Men cannot readily do the same with aspects of the feminine: they cannot wear dresses, skirts or women's jewelry without feeling "weird," even in many "liberated" circles of society. Men do not easily turn their intelligence to complex household tasks such as cleaning and health management of the family. Unlike women, who can and do embrace the masculine in themselves, men in our society do not readily embrace the feminine.

Male dominance in decision making and status positions furthers the exclusion of the feminine from masculine gender identity. As long as males dominate in arenas of social power—from the family to the larger institutions—and as long as they exclude women and the feminine from these realms, they will bind their identity to the "superior" attributes of the masculine. As long as female power remains limited in our society to care-giving, emotional concerns and the realm of relationship, and remains unrewarded in terms of status, decision-making power and material or symbolic gains (such as money), people will not be free to develop a human identity in a healthy way. At present, both girls and boys identify with the "superior" masculine attributes and activities of being objective, reasonable, powerful, analytical and strong. In order to belong to the female gender, girls are compelled to identify with being sensitive, dependent and emotional. Their identification with "inferior" feminine qualities often comes at the psychological expense of low self-esteem because these qualities are associated in our society with weakness.

Placing a sacred trust in reason, glorifying objectivity and worshipping science are preoccupations of modern society for both males and females. Many of the problems and dangers of our contemporary culture, therefore, can be understood in light of the ideal masculine gender identity and the corresponding devaluation of the feminine. Witness our penchant for distant warfare and aggression against strangers; we are reluctant to show hurt and sadness openly, while we express aggression and dominance publicly and without shame. Popular male heroes from James Bond to Woody Allen are detached self-observers who can always cover themselves with a good rational explanation, even if the explanation is a neurotic rationalization. We have few, if any, viable role models for men filling roles of wife and mother. Moreover, we rarely ask "Why?" but simply accept the fact that only women can fill both masculine and feminine roles. Because we have come to lend our primary public trust as a society to the "cold, hard facts" of science, we fail to listen to the many informing voices that other cultures know about. We have no ear for the voices of the earth, animals and natural elements. Our relation to the cosmos is mediated by facts about "energies," "holes" and "big bangs." While these notions may sound mythological, they are not experienced as myths which can guide human conduct and express mystery.

Our men, who assume the roles of partner and father in the family, often do so in confusion and without the ability to respond to the women and children around them. In couple psychotherapy, my co-therapist and I have come to notice a common inability among men to listen with understanding or empathy to simple emotional communications. Instead, they drift off into their own musings or defensive arguments and refuse to understand anything but a rational, sequential account of "what happened" or "what can be done."

We are ready, now, to turn to the story of Sir Gawain and the Lady Ragnell, which poses the question: "What do women really want?" This question, more than any other, provides a guide for us in doing therapy with couples who have lost basic attachment and trust in their relationships. Furthermore, it is a question which can lead us to the liberation and revaluing of the feminine both inside and out, in ourselves and in the lives of all men and women, for it directs us to the very heart of our humanity, to a concern for intimate relationship. Our failures in family making (not to be understood as the nuclear family ideal), our waste of human, animal and other natural resources, our despair about cooperating with human beings in other societies, and our oppression of our own partners and friends all reflect our devaluing of ordinary care-giving. Even the massive defensiveness of nuclear weaponry (ironically, the name for weapons is the same as the name of our basic family system) is part and parcel of the masculine mode of distancing and lack of relationship to self and other. But the prospect of nuclear holocaust is not a "men's problem," just as the kitchen and children are not "women's work." The reality and prospect of distant warfare, the dominance of white males in decision-making roles, and the concerns of ordinary living belong to all of us. At this time when our basic attachment to other human beings has too often worn thin, let us see what we can learn from an old folktale.[7]

Sir Gawain and the Lady Ragnell: What Do Women Really Want?

One day King Arthur is out hunting in the North, in Inglewood Forest, where he stalks a white hart until he wounds it with an arrow. Just as he goes to gather his kill, a monstrous fellow steps out of the woods. He calls himself "Sir Gromer Somer Jour" and threatens Arthur instantly with death by his ax. Shaken and confused, Arthur responds that he is unarmed for battle, and Sir Gromer grants him a twelve-month span in which to answer a riddle or return for his death blow. King Arthur departs this encounter entirely crestfallen and confused about the intent of the riddle.

When he arrives back at the castle, only Sir Gawain, among the Knights of the Round Table, can elicit the story of the adventure from the king. Reluctantly, Arthur describes the details of his confusing encounter and ends with great perplexity about the riddle posed by Sir Gromer. Gromer has asked Arthur to answer correctly the question, "What is it that women most desire, above all else?"

Both Gawain and Arthur suspect this question is a trick because it seems so inconsequential. Gawain is optimistic, however, saying, "After all, we have an entire year to collect answers throughout the kingdom. Surely someone will know." Arthur is less certain.

For an entire year, Arthur and his companions set about gathering data in their notebooks, asking the question of a broad and diverse sample of their population. Ultimately, they come together and compare notes, Gawain feeling certain that one of the answers will be right. Arthur doubts and worries, secretly assuming that no answer can be found to such a ridiculous question. With only a few days to go, he meanders again into Inglewood Forest, not too far from the place he originally shot the hart.

Out of the woods scrambles a hideous old hag who introduces herself as "the Lady Ragnell." She challenges Arthur, saying she *knows* he does not have the right answer to the riddle. Arthur is astounded at her officious manner, and replies that he cannot see how she might be concerned with his business. "The impudence of the woman!" is all he can think. Ragnell presses forward with a confidence that is startling to the king. She insists that only *she* can offer the correct response since she is the stepsister of Sir Gromer and privy to information that Arthur does not have.

Himself unconvinced of the answers he has collected, Arthur finally responds by offering her land, gold or jewels for the right answer. Ragnell refuses his material rewards, replying, "What use do I have for gold or jewels?" and asserts that only one thing will do: "If your nephew Gawain agrees to marry me, I will tell you the correct answer. That is my condition." Arthur says that Gawain is not his to give, that Gawain is his own free man. Ragnell replies that she is not asking for Arthur to give her Gawain; she is only asking him to propose the matter to Gawain and to discover what Gawain chooses to do, of his own free will.

Although Arthur asserts that he cannot put his nephew on the spot in this way, he immediately goes back to the castle and makes the proposal. Seeing his uncle almost groveling before him, Gawain cannot but take pity on the poor king and vows that he would wed the Devil himself in order to save the king's life. Together they go back to Ragnell and Gawain agrees to marry her if the answer she gives them is the one that saves the king's life.

On the appointed day, Arthur and Gawain ride solemnly out to meet the monstrous Sir Gromer. With his sword raised and his eye glinting, Gromer listens to Arthur read off the answers the two men collected in their research. None of them is the right one, and just as Gromer is about to let fall his ax, Arthur blurts out Ragnell's response to the question: "What women desire, above all else, is the power of sovereignty, the right to govern their own lives!"

At this Gromer dashes off, spitting hateful remarks about Ragnell and screaming that Arthur could never have found that answer on his own.

Arthur, Gawain and Ragnell ride back to the castle in silence. Only Lady Ragnell is in good spirits. There follows a great wedding banquet attended by the lords and ladies of the castle. Everyone is uncomfortable, squirming and commenting on the ugliness and bad manners of the bride. Ragnell, however, is unabashed; she eats heartily and appears to have a very good time.

In the wedding chamber later that evening, Ragnell seems pleased with Gawain's responses to her. "You have treated me with dignity," she says. "You have been neither repulsed nor pitying in your concern for me. Come kiss me now."

Gawain steps forward and kisses her on the lips and lo!, there stands a lovely and graceful woman with beautiful grey eyes. She turns round before him and queries, "Do you prefer me in this, my true form, or in my former shape?" "Well, of course in this shape, I mean, what . . . what a beautiful woman you are!" Gawain stammers. Then he leaps back with a challenge: "What manner of sorcery is this? What is going on here?"

Lady Ragnell explains that her brother had cursed her for being so bold as to disobey his orders. His curse was that she should appear as a loathsome hag until the greatest knight in all of Britain willingly agreed to marry her. Arthur's mistake of hunting in Inglewood Forest (the land Arthur had given to Gawain, but which rightfully belonged to Sir Gromer) was her first opportunity to be in contact with the king and to try to break Sir Gromer's vengeful spell.

Overjoyed, Gawain rushes toward his bride, crying, "You have done it! You have freed yourself from your brother's angry spell and now you are my own lovely bride!"

"Wait!" Ragnell interrupts, "I must tell you that only part of the curse is broken. You now have a choice to make, my friend. I can be in this my true shape during the day, in the castle, and take my other form at night in our chamber—or I can be in my true shape at night, in our bed, and in my former ugly shape by day in the castle. You cannot have it both ways. Think carefully before you choose."

Gawain falls silent, pondering the intent of the question, but only for a moment. "It is your choice, Ragnell, because it involves your life. Only you can decide," is his answer.

With this, Ragnell becomes radiant with joy and ease. She says, "My dear Gawain, you have answered well, because now the spell is entirely broken. The final condition was that if, after I became the bride of the greatest knight, he freely gave me sovereignty over my own life, I could return to my true form. Now I am free to be beautiful by day and beautiful by night."

Thus began the marriage of Sir Gawain and the Lady Ragnell.

The Challenge to Change

Some of the more entertaining and illuminating themes of this delightful story are obscure to a contemporary audience. For example, the character of the hag was probably well known to a fifteenth-century listener in terms of her specific psychology. The hag is a "loathsome lady"—dramatic, ugly and overwhelming. She is magically powerful in that she can ride men or children through the skies at night, under her own powers, and leave them exhausted or dead in the morning. Usually she is extraordinarily fat, broader than she is high, and is covered with warts and other unattractive growths, topped off with matted and grotesque coifs that are sometimes described as "green weedy hair." Her appearance and actions are not as serious as her magical power (in fact, her actions are often humorous). She is equipped to suck out the soul of a person who kisses her on the lips, and just looking directly in her eyes sets up a dangerous potential for soul-stealing. From these features, we can appreciate the heroism of Gawain in embracing and kissing the Lady Ragnell as readily as he did. If she were a real hag, her kiss could have brought him death. Finally, the hag does not weep real tears. She only pretends to cry, while she expresses her distress through malicious laughter and disdain or contempt. Clearly, no one can embrace a hag unless he has a lot of courage, and Gawain shows himself a great hero in saving his uncle's life as he did.

Secondly, Gawain and Arthur were also well-known characters from a variety of popular stories and ballads. Just as most of us know James Bond and Woody Allen as figures of contemporary American culture, so the fifteenth-century audience would know Arthur and Gawain. Arthur was a rational hero; he was strong and proud, though sometimes an overly conservative king. In this story, as in some other ballads, Arthur is a bit of a fretting and dottering old man. Sometimes Arthur is made to play the comical figure of the old patriarch who stays in the background as he encourages the younger knights to "go out there and fight." Arthur cherishes his relationship with his nephew Gawain, and frequently relies on Gawain's virtues to be "purer" than his own.

Gawain, as a collective image, expresses some of the courtly ideals for knights of the medieval period. In his famous encounter with the Green Knight, for example, Gawain remains brave and courteous, careful of women's feelings and steadfast in his loyalties, showing just a bit of weakness or vulnerability (for example, in flinching before the stroke of the Green Knight and in his acceptance of some of the seductive "gifts" of the Green Knight's wife). The combination of emotional vulnerability and knightly courage was a special blend in the courtly lover. More than in later periods of English culture, the medieval period celebrated male-female relationships, in both sacred and secular contexts, as the "heart" of human culture.[8] Gawain is a recognized type of medieval hero, perhaps closer to Woody Allen than to James Bond, but different from any of our predominantly rational male figures. He could give himself over to his emotions and respond empathically, willingly and vulnerably to a woman's pain or personal invitation. A popular modern figure who conveys something of Gawain's nature is Zorba in Kazantzakis's *Zorba the Greek*. Gawain was not as lusty or passionate as Zorba, but he had a soft spot for women's experience and remained open to influence beyond his rational ideals. Generally, Gawain emerges from the tests of his knightly valor victorious or only slightly scathed, as with the Green Knight.

From the point of view of Jungian psychology, I interpret Arthur and Gawain to be fused together in one heroic posture, until the end of the story and the resolution of the spell. Gawain represents openness, courage and the willingness to go forth into the darkness of an unknown challenge as a conscious hero (i.e., by his own free will). What Gawain lacks are good judgment, maturity and objectivity. Arthur completes Gawain as a heroic figure in that he provides the requisite objectivity and authority of the patriarch. As king, Arthur is traditional, powerful, rational and conservative. He adheres to heroic ideals as principles of the head, rather than of the heart. Arthur is dependent on Gawain's enthusiasm and optimism in the face of danger. Gawain's enthusiasm and optimism are, in turn, dependent on the authority and approval of the king. Clearly, it would not be sensible to marry the Devil for any reason other than saving the king's head. Arthur and Gawain together make a complete hero, one able to solve problems rationally *and* act according to an ideal code. Until Gawain is faced with the hag directly, in his own wedding chamber separate from Arthur, he does not understand the dimension of sorcery into which he has enthusiastically entered. Without the real meaning of the challenge clear to him, Gawain is fused with Arthur (and the tradition of the patriarchy). Only Ragnell can free Gawain from Arthur and truly make him "his own man."

In our first look at the story, we should also note the theme of anger in the face of loss. Recall Sir Gromer's angry confrontation with Arthur, Ragnell's with Arthur, Gawain's with Ragnell and, finally, Ragnell's forthright challenge of Gawain. *The challenge to change in the face of loss* is the central emotional motif of the story. This motif emerges in individual development in middle life, when people commonly confront unexpected loss for the first time in facing death, divorce, desertion, illness or the departure of children. Death or illness in aging parents, the problems and limits of personal health, and separation through divorce make up the kinds of shocking losses that bring people to psychotherapy in middle life.

Jung maintained that the task of development in middle life lies in counterbalancing the one-sidedness of one's earlier life. For men, this usually involves the need to integrate into personal identity the "repressed feminine" aspects of their own personality, called the *anima*. Women generally need to integrate the "repressed masculine" or *animus*. Development in middle and later life would thus consist of changing one's earlier adaptation and consciously including much of what had previously been experienced as habit and dependency on others.

For men, Jung assumed that middle life development entailed moving from being an aloof and distant "hero" to the acknowledgment of one's dependence on others and the importance of relationships. For women, the situation would be the opposite: development would require a shift from an accommodative and dependent identity to a more autonomous and independent one. Cross-cultural studies done by David Gutmann on ego styles among people in several European and non-European cultures appear to substantiate Jung's claim of a shift in adaptation in later life.[9] Gutmann's findings show that men tend to shift from an active style of "mastery" in early life to a more passive style of "accommodation" in later life. Women shift from a passive-accommodative ego style to more active mastery. Gutmann's research did not give central consideration to conscious identity or self-concept. Jung's psychology stresses that developmental shifts in personal style must take place in consciousness, in one's personal awareness, in order for one to benefit from individual development as fully as possible. Circumstances which demand new adaptations can change a person's method of coping—a woman, for example, might change from depending on a man's financial support to earning her own living—but changes in adaptation do not always alter one's attitude toward life. Jung's concept of *individuation,* which entails the successive integration of previously repressed or habituated aspects of the personality, emphasizes integration through consciousness as the key to successful psychological development.

Using the story, we begin in therapy with the problem of "recognition of potential loss." Arousing people's motivation to work on inner issues which have led to stagnation, and are now blocking trust, is the first step in this kind of couple therapy. "Embracing the hag" initially entails coming to terms with what is dark and frightening in oneself so that one can release the partner from the burden of carrying one's own resentment, frustration and despair. Each person needs to recognize and sort through resistance and fear of change, her or his own repressions, and the dominance of particular aspects of one's own self.

The problem of confronting and embracing the disappointments and frustrations in oneself can be conceptualized as a process of differentiating between the concerns of attachment and those of dominance within the couple relationship. When a distressed couple enters therapy (usually through the wife's insistence or because a child has "brought" the couple to therapy by acting out), the partners are usually operating out of a "dominance-submission" posture rather than an "attachment-separation" one. The basic mode of intimate relationship is the instinctual pattern of attachment and separation. When this pattern, with its expressive gestures, symbolic meanings and recurring actions, is abandoned in favor of a dominance pattern or "power struggle," each person feels threatened and depressed on a day-to-day basis. Instead of the two people relating emotionally as interdependent individuals with the ability to see and satisfy each other's needs, they relate as a symbiotic or fused unit in which one person is "on top" and the other is "underneath"; there is a constant power struggle on every issue.

Although the two people may recognize the non-rational nature of their struggle (e.g., they may say, "It's ridiculous, but we just can't stop fighting over petty matters"), they feel it is impossible to stop struggling. Until both people face the meaning of dominance and submission in their relationship, which almost always involves the devaluing of the feminine, they cannot shift their concerns to attachment. Confrontation with the potential loss in their situation, through the therapists' backing and elaborating the voice of the hag, often moves people out of the power struggle that had been so prominently in the center. This is just the first step in working through the dominance and submission concerns, however.

Paradoxically, confrontation with loss, resentment and frustration can open the doors to the next stage of development for each person. For both, the next stage typically involves revaluing the feminine. For the man, this process consists of claiming his own dependency, fears, needs and feelings, and expressing these openly. For the woman, the process involves claiming the worth and authority of her own perspective and integrating confidence into her self-image as a competent individual who has developed skills as a caregiver. For each person individually, embracing the resented, shameful and undervalued "hag" can result in the discovery of new vitality —a previously disguised "princess" with clear grey eyes and a graceful demeanor.

2

Feminism and the Psychology of C.G. Jung

When I speak about feminism and Jung's psychology in the same breath, I am often challenged by colleagues, especially those in social work, who contend that Jung's theory is misogynist. Feminists generally have been critical of Jung's work and of the contributions of contemporary Jungians to women's psychology. Many useful critiques of Jungian psychology have been written from a feminist perspective, and we need to continue to be skeptical about applying androcentric concepts to women.[1] Androcentrism, or reasoning from the perspective of a male, has been a problem in Jungian psychology as it has been in all other major psychodynamic theories in psychology. As women have begun to validate the worth and truth of their own experiences, they have discovered that many traditional concepts about their motivations and desires are constraining and distorting.

A concept such as "penis envy," which implies that a woman has a hole where a penis should be, is an immediately understandable illustration of androcentrism in generally accepted psychoanalytic theory. An anxious middle-aged woman, identified with the idea that she is inferior intellectually, may be called "animus-ridden" by a Jungian psychotherapist because she speaks in an opinionated and insistent manner about a general or vague idea. This kind of labeling can be considered androcentric when it arises from essentially male standards that are applied to the woman's experience without accounting for her social context or the character of female gender identity and traditional sex roles.

Jung's concepts of the anima, or repressed feminine, in men and the animus, or repressed masculine, in women are particularly vulnerable to being considered androcentric by feminists. Jung referred to these concepts typically as *archetypes*, but sometimes as *complexes*. Either way, he conceived of them as natural predispositions to respond to the opposite sex in particular ways and to behave in particular ways regarding the domain of the opposite sex. In Jung's descriptions of the anima, he tended to confuse the experience of the female, from a male's point of view, with actual women. Rather than distinguishing explicitly between men's fears and fantasies about women, and actual women, Jung tended to confuse the fantasied and the real. Consider the following passage:

So far as my experience goes, a man always understands fairly easily

23

what is meant by the anima; indeed, as I said, he frequently has a quite definite picture of her, so that from a varied collection of women of all periods he can single out the one who comes closest to the anima-type.[2]

The continuing confusion between a man's predisposition to regard women in a particular way, and a woman's actual personality has resulted in some Jungian typologies for women which are based on anima-types in men.[3]

Jung derived the concept of the animus in women from his discovery of the anima in men. "Since the anima is an archetype that is found in men," he writes, "it is reasonable to suppose that an equivalent archetype must be present in women."[4] After making this statement, Jung goes on to disclaim that he simply "deduced" the animus without clinical experience of women. He remains baffled, however, about the animus concept since, as he says, "I have never met any woman who could tell me anything definite about his personality."[5] Because Jung did not attend to the social context of the development of anima and animus, nor to the ramifications of sole mothering by females, he could not elaborate convincing reasons why men projected such a singular and personal image of anima (as woman) whereas women did not project a singular, personal image of animus (as man).

Not only did Jung conceptualize these ideas primarily from a male perspective, but he contributed to much popular thinking about the inferiority of women's moral and intellectual capacities. The woman possessed by her animus is described as "obstinate, harping on principles, laying down the law, dogmatic, world-reforming, theoretic, word-mongering, argumentative, and domineering."[6] When this kind of description is taken seriously and applied to women who are already anxious about their intellectual capacities, a woman can feel defeated from the outset.[7]

Despite the androcentrism of some Jungian concepts, Jung's theories and methods provide unique means for understanding symbolic expressions and for transcending personal loss. A feminist approach to therapy using Jungian psychology is easily accessible and is consistent with Jung's theory of psychic development, as I will show here.

Feminist Theory and Therapy

First let me clarify what I mean by a "feminist approach" or "feminist therapy." I am a self-declared feminist, and my therapeutic work is consistent with feminist therapy.[8] This is part of my identity as a psychologist and psychotherapist because of my concern for engendering greater authority, autonomy, competence and independence in women as complete human beings. The attainment of personal authority is a difficult process for women in our culture. A woman's struggle for authority must be interpreted within the context of her female gender identity. The particular aspects of inferiority, weakness and stupidity associated with the gender attributes of the female are special concerns in developing female authority. To have a position of personal authority as a woman, rather than identifying with the personal authority of men, one has to come to terms with the social meanings of gender and understand these in context. Developing female authority is an ongoing struggle in a society which discriminates against women's independence.

As a feminist therapist, I am committed to assisting everyone—both men and women—in revaluing the ordinary tasks of life, in maintaining intimate relationships and in providing care. This was from the beginning a personal, ethical commitment on my part; it was not part of my formal training. What I have discovered in my work in empowering women and revaluing relational ideals is that all of us are constantly influenced by unconscious sex-role stereotyping and sexual bias. Because white men dominate the decision-making arenas of our society, and because the "inferior" qualities of dependence, emotionality, etc., are associated with female gender identity, we must be alert to the assumptions of any conceptual scheme we use to describe identity in women or to characterize what is feminine.

Women consistently face a double bind when they speak with authority or insistence. As discovered by Broverman et al., the ideal man in our society is assumed to be more competent, more independent, more objective and more logical than the ideal woman.[9] The ideal woman is imagined as more submissive, more dependent and less objective than a "healthy adult" (sex unspecified). The double bind in a woman's authority is therefore obvious. If a woman assumes the objectivity, competence and independence of a healthy adult, she is censured for not being feminine. If she identifies with the submissive, dependent and more passive qualities of being feminine, she has failed to become an adult. In regard to identifying herself as a competent, confident authority figure, a woman cannot win. Hence, the unintegrated animus of an opinionated woman may be more the product of conflict in social attributions about women's rights to authority than it is a product of a woman's psychology.

That even psychologists expect women to be more passive and dependent than men, and less objective than healthy adults, has been convincingly demonstrated.[10] Such sexual stereotyping, while it may be acknowledged as harmful by individuals, continues to be accepted by large segments of our society. Perhaps even more important, stereotypical masculine traits are regarded as more desirable than stereotypical feminine traits. Both men and women incorporate into their self-concepts the stereotyped attributes of their gender identity. The tendency for women to denigrate themselves can be understood as social pressure to conform to a negative self-concept. The inferior status of women's gender identity has been substantiated in a number of well-designed, broad-based studies which followed the work of Broverman et al.[11]

Some of Jung's ideas, especially the idea of archetypes, have been used to reinforce the internalization of "inferior" identity. Jung's ideas of archetype, archetypal masculine and feminine principles, as well as the concepts of anima and animus, can be used for misogynist purposes by implying that women's identities must be constricted in particular ways.[12] Anthony Stevens's treatise on archetypes is a recent example of misogynist reasoning about the archetypal feminine and archetypal masculine, leading him to pronouncements about women's biological destiny to mother and nurture.[13] Until men personally embrace the concerns of care-giving and relationship, they cannot presume expertise in the question of who should stay at home or what skills are involved in care-giving.

The first premise of feminist therapy, as I see it, is to examine a person's current conscious attitude about life in light of the "inferior" attributes of female gender. Specifically, I pose this question: How much has the person connected female identity with "less than" attributes—less powerful, less objective, less intelligent, weaker, less rational and the like? An examination of the underlying assumptions of gender identity, in the context of a patriarchal culture, is always a part of my assessment of a woman's or a man's sense of personal competence and self-worth.

Secondly, from a feminist perspective, I consider the endeavor of psychotherapy to be a collaborative process within a particular social ritual. Meeting in the same setting, at regular times, paying a set fee, and thinking of the therapist as the expert are parts of the general ritual associated with therapy. This ritual can take on the meaning of the medical model of diagnosis and treatment, of discovering the "deficit" and rooting it out. The ritual can also take on the meaning of confession or an educational venture. I prefer to define the therapy ritual primarily as a "consultation" which is educational, discovery-oriented and interpersonally powerful. Because therapy combines empathy and objectivity, it is a unique intimate encounter.

I see therapeutic consultation, then, as a collaborative, interactive process which is shaped consciously by the client's concerns and desires. The ideals of collaboration between or among competent people, free flow of information and reciprocity of mutual trust (not just an exchange of one thing for something else) are my general guides. Consequently, I adhere to feminist ethics regarding the responsibility of therapists and rights of clients by clarifying my own training and credentials, refraining from routinely interpreting client criticism as "resistance" (or some other convenient label), informing clients of alternatives to psychotherapy and of the potentially harmful side effects of therapy.[14]

*

With the collaborative process as my ideal, the following basic strategies for change are the fundamental "action plans" that underlie all techniques I use:

1) *Management of therapeutic relationship:* facilitating rapport and then mediating or managing it to support changes sought by client (e.g., using "transference" and "therapeutic alliance").

2) *Meaning reconstruction:* facilitating attitudinal change in client in terms of assumptions, expectations, fantasies, etc., which have limited personal identity, agency, responsibility; expansion of the personal meaning sphere (e.g., using interpretation or paradoxical interventions).

3) *New learning:* collaborating in the business of developing new skills, modes of action and competence in interacting with the environment, especially the interpersonal environment (e.g., behavioral techniques or "homework").

4) *Expansion of vocabulary for meaning making:* teaching client new words and modes of meaning making to develop greater clarity and freedom in understanding human motivations, responsibility, agency and empathy in personal and interpersonal life (e.g., teaching the words and ideas of dream interpretation to client).

Jungian methods fill out these basic strategies in ways which are quite compatible with feminist therapy, provided we clarify the use of certain theoretical concepts as they impinge on technique. Jung's contributions to the practice of psychotherapy are both revolutionary and frequently misunderstood. As a feminist and a Jungian, I focus on four particular contributions made by Jung in the work I do in analysis and psychotherapy: the need to reconstruct the dominant conscious attitude, the importance of reclaiming animus and anima projections, the individuation process and the idea of competing realities in the interactional field (both interpersonal and intrapsychic). Each of these will now be examined in turn.

Reconstructing the Dominant Conscious Attitude

Jung's emphasis on the current dominant attitude of consciousness as the field or focus for therapeutic influence fits well with feminist therapy. Feminist therapists assist their clients in an ongoing examination of assumptions about self and other in relationship, especially with regard to unconscious attributions of inferiority or superiority based on gender identity.

In 1929 Jung wrote, "Neurosis or any other mental conflict depends much more on the personal attitude of the patient than on his infantile history," and, "The task of psychotherapy is to correct the conscious attitude."[15] A focus on the present and actual attitude of the client directs primary attention to "person-in-situation," as social workers refer to the contextual setting of a person's life. I emphasize the influence of the intrapsychic and interpersonal fields as they appear in significant relationships between the client and the people in her or his life, including the therapeutic relationship. I also emphasize the influences of the dominant (i.e., white American) and immediate (e.g., Hispanic-American) cultures on the interpersonal field.

My use of Jung's idea of psychological complexes is the extension of a practical emphasis on the current attitude in the intrapsychic and interpersonal fields. A complex is a collection of images, ideas and feelings that is compelling or motivating in a non-rational way. A complex, such as that organized around the body-image experience of "I," may be conscious or only partly conscious due to its familiarity. A complex such as that organized around the excluded aspects of one's gender may be wholly unconscious.

The experience of a complex in interpersonal relating is that of an habitual field of action, symbol and emotion organized around a core of meaning, in relation to some typical aspect of human life. Examples of ordinary complexes in everyday living are "I," "mother," "father," "child" and "hero." These complexes are not rationally discrete entities, but states of being that are enacted in typical ways. The idea of complexes is especially useful for understanding non-rational communication in an interpersonal situation, between two persons or in a group such as a family. Unconscious complexes can interfere with intentional and rational means of relating; they interfere with being a person and seeing the other as a person.

When a complex is experienced solely within an individual, it is experienced as an inner conflict, a conflict between complexes, so to speak. Usually the conflict is between the personal ego complex or "I" as an intentional actor and some other less conscious complex.

When an <u>unconscious complex is being enacted, a person feels</u> "beside oneself"; she or he feels strange moods, anxieties and/or ideas that seem exaggerated and unfounded. When a complex endures, it is typically being enacted within an interpersonal field, that is, between persons. The initiator expresses the complex in some way which is picked up and played out by someone else.

For example, a young woman may be talking with a young man in a rational and intentional way. Suddenly she starts tidying up around him and telling him how he feels and what he is thinking. In effect, she is organizing his reality as if she were a mother; she has been "overtaken" by the mother complex. She implies by her behavior that she will nurture him and organize him. If the man in this situation responds by backing away and being aloof, he is saying, in effect, "You are treating me like a baby. Let me alone." The woman may then respond by trying to repair the communication between them, anxiously feeling that she has made some mistake. To her anxious response, he reacts with increased distancing. The two would then be off and running in their enactment of a negative mother complex, in which he would behave as the overwhelmed boy toward an engulfing mother, and she would begin to believe, fearfully, that she is bad, that her care-giving or words are bad. If the two of them continue to enact this non-rational complex, they will find the syntactical meaning of their words confusing; they will no longer be communicating as intentional persons.

The negative mother complex, a common cultural problem associated with female identity, is organized around the archetype of the Terrible Mother. By this archetype I mean the instinctual-emotional pattern of human behaviors and expressions associated with the destructive and overwhelming aspects of nurturance. The Terrible Mother is imaged as a savage goddess, a witch or a hag. These archetypal images are associated with death, suffocation, stagnation, symbiosis and fear of incorporation. The epidemic proportions of the negative mother complex in our society are rooted in our collective condition of devaluing nurturant, attachment activities and assigning these activities solely to women, without giving them tangible rewards.

I have introduced the idea of archetype, and by implication the idea of the collective unconscious, without making my meaning entirely clear. Consistent with Jung's definition of the archetype *an sich* (as such), I use the term to mean *a pattern of action and thought which organizes human instinctual-emotional responses (expressed in gesture or symbol) in relationship*. Relationship may consist of an intrapsychic interchange between complexes (conscious and unconscious part-personalities) as in a dream, or it may consist of an interpersonal relationship between people. Jung's idea of the archetype as an organizing form for instinctual response is compatible with Bowlby's concept of human instinct as a behavioral pattern which has become centrally built into our species for survival purposes.[16] Human instincts are not simply spontaneous impulses, but are patterned behaviors which emerge only in the appropriate social environments to which they correspond. Instincts in primates and humans are less fixed, more flexible, take longer to develop and are more variably expressed than those in less complex animals.

Human instincts are social in nature in that they regulate the relationships between members of the species. In both Jung's theory of archetypes and Bowlby's theory of human instinct, typical emotional response patterns arise at certain points in the human life cycle and concern communications essential to survival needs. These patterns are concerned with activities such as infant bonding, peer play, territorial curiosity, hierarchical dominance, initiation rituals, adult bonding and territorial aggression. Jung said the following of archetype in relation to instinct in humans:

> Instincts are by no means blind, spontaneous, isolated impulses; they are on the contrary associated with typical situational patterns and cannot be released unless existing conditions correspond to the *a priori* pattern. The collective contents expressed in mythologems represent such situational patterns [i.e., archetypes], which are so intimately connected with the release of instinct. For this reason, knowledge of them is of the highest practical importance to the psychotherapist.[17]

Anthony Stevens has argued for the superiority of Jung's concept of archetype over Bowlby's instinct in that Jung's idea includes the symbolic expression connected to the typical social instincts of people, the symbolizing animals.[18] States of emotional arousal—for example, fear, attachment and separation—are symbolized in traditional stories and human rituals, and are expressed individually in gesture and language. The archetype *as such* is evidenced as integrated patterns of physiological arousal and gestural expression. The archetype *as such* is further to be found in the typical motifs and themes of traditional stories, myths and rituals across cultures. The range of potential human expression of instinctual response, through meaning, is much greater than that of other animals. What it *means* to feel angry, loving or fearful, under particular human relational conditions, is expressed in typical and similar imagistic ways by people in different societies and cultures.

For my purposes in therapy of working on the current conscious attitude, I regard the archetype as *an inherent organizing form for the expression of what is enduring and archaic in human nature.* When archetypal experiences and their expression in complexes, especially unconscious complexes, are distinguished for the client from ordinary reality, the result is generally a great sense of relief. The client understands that archetypal images and meaning are "bigger than life" and more powerful than an ordinary person; gods, goddesses and divine forces are not within the realm of personal responsibility. People necessarily engage in archetypal feelings and images, but they cannot control such realities or expressions in the way people control a sequential, rational narrative. Complexes are infused with meaning that is emotionally powerful and typically implied rather than made specific. Complexes, like schemata or "pre-operational" thought (in Piaget's terms), are non-rational expressions. They are organized in image-affect fields of thought and activity which are patterned and can be recognized and understood, but not through rational means.

The negative mother complex again provides a good specific illustration. Organized around the archetype of the Terrible Mother, this complex expresses the instinctual-emotional response to the negative aspects of nurturing or attachment. Incorporation, suffocation, stagnation and fears of them are all experienced in this complex. The complex is imaged as the witch, hag or savage goddess. Each of these figures is far meaner, uglier and more powerfully wicked than any ordinary woman could be. When the complex is attributed to a woman, or when a woman feels identified with the complex, she experiences herself as having more power than she rationally knows she has. She condemns herself for flaws which are then exaggerated and beyond the responsibility of human beings. Long-term identification with the negative mother complex in an individual woman can result in a great deal of self-inflicted hatred and isolation.

The Animus and a Woman's Sense of Herself

The animus and anima of Jung's psychology are concepts which are sometimes considered archetypes and sometimes complexes.[19] I define them as complexes and find that my use of Jung's theory is more systematic from doing so. These contrasexual complexes are organized around the identity archetype of Not-I: the animus or anima is a complex of habitual actions, symbol, image and emotion organized around the core of Other or Not-I in regard to excluded aspects of gender identity. Elements excluded from one's gender identity, but experienced socially as essentially human in one's life context, make up the "content" of the contrasexual complex. Since these elements change in the course of development, the complex can be understood as responsive to both ongoing developmental changes in gender identity and to the social context of gender functions in any society. Gender attributions and identification may contain both masculine and feminine elements, but social gender categories are mutually exclusive. Assigning particular contents to the animus or anima can never be adequate to the range of experiences in the individual development of identity over a lifetime. Simply calling the animus "Logos" or "Spirit," or the anima "Eros" or "Soul," is thus too limiting for understanding experiences of these unconscious complexes that evolve during the course of life.

Before I turn to the scheme for animus development which I find useful in practice, I would like to review briefly a relevant definition of gender identity which arises out of recent studies in social psychology. Carolyn Sherif has worked out an adequate conceptual system which encompasses many aspects of the problem of gender. Here is a brief passage from her work on the meaning of gender:

> Gender is a scheme for social categorization of individuals, and every known society has some gender scheme. Every gender scheme recognizes biological differentiation while also creating social differentiation. . . . Gender categories are mutually exclusive, in the sense that social membership in one precludes membership in others.[20]

Sherif stresses that gender is a "self-system" involving internal conflicts and a psychological relationship to social categories, as well as varying knowledge of these categories. Gender is a multileveled identity concern, as are the animus and anima complexes. I have come to believe, from my clinical work, that sex biases and subtle social cues about gender are every bit as important to the content of animus and anima complexes as are the personal relationships with the mother and father, for example. Sometimes the dominant cultural context is even more important than personal relationships. Specifically, a single woman working as an executive among male colleagues will have certain animus themes whether or not her father provided a good role model and/or fathered her adequately.

As a woman's sense of self-as-female changes consciously, especially in regard to her self-esteem, she develops a new relationship to the animus, and the complex takes on new images. The development of the sense of being a person is always self-other development in the way that one responds to and anticipates both self and other. In other words, there is no such thing as an isolated sense of "self" or "ego" which evolves outside of relationship to "other." The other may be an intrapsychic complex or another person, but the state of "otherness" is experienced as different and discrete from "I." Consequently, one's relationship to the animus, and the relationship of animus to self, must be understood developmentally as taking on different forms and different dynamics. When I review developmental changes in psychotherapy, I look at current interpersonal relationships in the client's life, at the therapeutic relationship as a model of these other relationships and at apparent changes in self-esteem (from appearance, motivations and self-reports), as well as changes in dream material.

As we attempt in therapy to reconstruct the dominant conscious attitude, a major ongoing goal is the integration into consciousness of the unconscious complexes. Recognizing the complex, knowing its meaning, being able to talk about it and learning to penetrate its message are all means for expanding one's sense of self. A woman may project her animus complex or she may identify with it. Either way, when she is doing this unconsciously, she will not have its meaning and motivation at her own disposal. Psychotherapy does not bring "control" of complexes (they are non-rational and not subject to control), but it brings understanding of them so that they can be more closely integrated in oneself; one withdraws them from the environment and others, thereby lessening their habitual grip on identity. Recognizing that one is not a killer even though one sometimes feels like one (as do others) is one step in enlarging the current conscious attitude. Another is to understand when and why one may feel like killing something or someone. Integration of the animus thus results in greater personal freedom and in deeper empathy with others.

The animus development scheme included here is the basis for assessing women's vulnerabilities to particular projections and identity states in the current conscious attitude. It is presented in detail elsewhere, along with supporting clinical and theoretical material.[21] The scheme was developed by Florence Wiedemann and myself as a first attempt to examine the self-other process of change in animus relationship as we have experienced it in psychotherapy with women. I include the stages here, along with a dream to illustrate each one, because they demonstrate both the working of the complex according to Jungian psychology and how Jung's concepts can be revised and made compatible with feminist therapy. After I present the scheme, I will discuss the difference between a developmental difficulty of the animus and the role of hag in the negative mother complex in relationships. We have no comparable scheme for anima development in men, but much work has been done on anima images and can be considered to supplement the ideas presented here for women.

The stages are hypothesized from clinical experiences with women in psychotherapy and from theoretical stages of development from structural developmental theories in psychology, such as Jane Loevinger's stages of ego development.[22] Although no empirical investigation of these stages has been attempted, the sequencing of the self-animus themes has been helpful clinically and fits with common sense and women's felt experience. Whether or not individuals follow the sequence in some exact way matters less than the general usefulness of thinking about the past and the future in planning therapeutic interventions. Sequencing allows us to understand better what foundation of trust a person brings to therapy and what can be anticipated in the way of probable changes.

For the time being, these stages should be understood as formal or structural stages, each with an internal logic and imagery of its own. Theoretically, no stage can be skipped because the achievements of each new orientation are built on all that has come previously. Although these stages have a chronological "flavor," they are not bound to chronology: people do not necessarily develop as they age. We can stop developing at any point in the life cycle, and we can retreat to an earlier adaptation at any time, as we often do under stress. The earlier stages characterize patterns of relating to the animus that may seem immature for adulthood, but may still be adaptive in a particular life context. Since ideals for feminine gender identity include dependency and lack of objectivity, women can remain adaptive to life contexts as adults even when they are enacting child-like roles. Some of the early stages will be associated with such pathologies as psychosis and personality disorders.[23]

Each stage of animus development is characterized by identity complexes for self and animus. An individual may identify with any of the imagistic themes at a particular stage. Consciously or unconsciously, a person may shift back and forth between animus and woman identities, depending primarily on how the interpersonal arena stimulates intrapsychic realities. The animus, as a complex, can be understood as an affectively charged scheme that is activated as a woman relates to and fantasizes men, boys, male institutions and the more abstract "masculine" in her life. Each stage is characterized here by a mythological story, except the final one, for which we have no adequate story. All the stories are from Greek mythology, not because the Greeks have the most adequate system for feminine imagery, but because Greek mythology is the one system which is best known and probably exerts the greatest influence on our broad and diverse Judeo-Christian culture. Each dream illustration presented here comes from an adult woman (over twenty-one) in psychotherapy. The dreams are offered as images or samples of the feeling states and inner life of each stage.

Stages of Animus Development

1) Animus as Alien Other

The woman (or girl) feels contained in the world of sameness of mother or female. She is united, as a mother or daughter, in a maternal relationship or similar bond with a woman (or women). The strength of her identity and trust is in the female relationship. The animus is experienced as alien, primitive or abusive—e.g., the killer, rapist or primitive man. Affective response to the animus is basic mistrust.

Dream illustration: Someone is responsible for murders where the dreamer lives in a beautiful house as a starlet. The dreamer suspects it is a man who is big and frightening. She sees the man who terrifies her. His forehead is like a gorilla's and his eyes are darting around. He is very scared himself. She puts a coat hanger around his arms and hits him on the head two or three times. She says, "I know it is you," and the man says, "You knew it wouldn't be easy." He tries to get his arms out and there is a lot of blood. The dreamer is afraid he will kill her too. She pushes him down a circular hole that goes down a long ways. Then her father comes up and she says, "It is like *Mission Impossible* or a situation comedy." And she is afraid to be alone with her father.

Story: The Rape of Persephone
Identity images: Persephone, Demeter, Hades

2) Animus as Father, God, Patriarch

The woman experiences herself as being sacrificed to the world of the animus, father or men. She may be the "father's daughter" and take on qualities of the father or of the mother's animus. She may alternately protect the mother from the father or the father from the mother. She sacrifices her own individuality in living for masculine approval in some way, either through appearance (beautiful princess) or achievements (performance-oriented) or both. In this stage, the woman lives out either her father's aspirations or the animus of the mother—i.e., her mother's unlived creativity and sexuality. The woman feels a loss of genuineness, a sacrifice of her own authenticity or simply a constraint to make herself acceptable to men.

Her appearance or performance (e.g., looking good or having success) feels like a false cover over a flawed or inadequate self. She experiences herself as trying to please the patriarchal powers, which may be through being a "good wife and mother" or a "sexy lady" or a "good student or assistant." These covers have been designed to meet the requirements of father, God or king—as the way in which the institution of motherhood meets the demands of the patriarchy for servile support of the masculine domain. The woman knows, somehow, that she does not exist "in her own right." She feels "sanctioned" by powerful male authorities, and she functions often in fear and guilt regarding her animus. She may become depressed and apathetic if she remains at this stage over most of her adulthood, feeling that no one can save her real self, which is too lost or flawed.

Dream illustration: The dreamer is standing in a doorway of the farmhouse where she lives. She is looking through the glass into the backyard of the farm. Her best girlfriend stands in front of her, between her and the window. Outside, everything is a mauve fog and very eerie. The fog is moving about and some of it coalesces into a giant ghostly form. From the distance, the form moves toward the dreamer and her friend. It is huge and frightening. Just before it closes in on them, a voice says, "Destiny is a man." The friend drops dead. The dreamer awakens just before it gets to her because she knows she will die also.

Story: Pandora
Identity images: Pandora, Zeus, Hephaestus

3) Animus as Youth, Hero, Lover

The woman experiences herself as surrendering to the animus. This is more active than being sacrificed, and she feels more like she is entering into a relationship in a lively way. She may surrender to a man, an institution governed by men (e.g., graduate school), an ideal or a religion. She feels herself willingly swept away and actively wanting to give in. The initial phase of this stage is often marked by impersonal relationships with groups or gangs of men (in dream images or waking life). These men are reminiscent of the "son lovers" of the Great Mother figures: they are undifferentiated males (e.g., youthful lovers or professors). Initially, the woman greatly fears a "death marriage" or moving too quickly into the darkness. Eventually, she feels validated and completed by the animus if she has really made a partnership.

Still, her identity as woman is incomplete and largely reflected by the animus. Especially, her sense of competence and authority will continue to depend on men's reflections because she must be reflected in order to esteem herself. Anger finally emerges as she confronts the buried feminine aspects of her own womanly self and/or those of the women around her. She is confronted by a rage and fury that are imaged by the great goddesses underground, such as the Furies. (The woman may retreat to Stage 1 either permanently or temporarily at this point. Temporary retreat often seems necessary and effective for further development.)

Dream illustration: The dreamer has taken her lover, a young man, away from another woman. They kiss passionately. He lifts her off the ground. He doesn't look quite like himself (in waking life). He is taller and more handsome. He feels so strong and this seems awe-inspiring to the crowd. The crowd has grown silent watching. She and her lover are going to leave together as a couple, but before they do so the dreamer's old aunt takes off her wig and shows her matted hair underneath.

Story: Amor and Psyche
Identity images: Psyche, Amor, Venus

4) Animus as Partner Within

The woman experiences herself as re-membered. She has recovered her consciousness as a strong and competent woman and has the feeling of being vitally reborn. What was passively acted out or projected, in terms of authority and competence in herself, is now experienced and actively pursued. She is industrious in her work and relationships in a way she feels is entirely new and exciting. She feels her own agency without oppressive concerns for approval and reflection from men or other authority figures. She is able to see herself and other women realistically in a broad social context. Perhaps for the first time, she can empathize with women in their dependency needs and their compensatory control (which she previously abhorred). She turns her attention more toward embracing the "life of a woman," often by supporting other women and cherishing friendships with women and neglected aspects of herself.

Dream illustration: The dreamer climbs a very steep cliff face. It is all sand so that when she puts her hand out to pull herself up, the face of the cliff just crumbles. Finally she gets the knack of the climb, however, and makes it up to a plateau. The sand is orangish brown and she is at first repulsed by the color. She hates the color because she hates the anguish of the climb and never wants to see this place again. When she arrives at the top, her parents are there and so is a huge model of a woman's body. The model is made from the same golden sand, only now the sand seems beautiful and golden. The dreamer says, "I think it was huge, the model, but I think it was me."

The scene changes and the dreamer is in an episode of *Bonanza*. She is a beautiful dance-hall girl who is lynched at the center of town. She is hanging on a structure of charred and burned wood, fully conscious. Little Joe rescues her, untying her and lifting her up. He carries her to a hotel and asks for two rooms. The dreamer listens carefully to discover whether or not he will respect her and ask for a separate room, rather than assume they will have sex together. She is happy to find that he respects her. In the final episode of the dream, the dreamer discovers that she might have a penis, that she is partly male or masculine, and she is quite curious about this. She has pretended not to know it.

Story: Ariadne and Dionysus
Identity images: Ariadne, Theseus, Dionysus, Minotaur

5) Animus as Androgyne

The exceptional woman experiences herself as fully integrated in the sense that she is "fully human," both in terms of competence and self-esteem and in terms of compassion and a vivid and diverse feeling life. She has an objective understanding of men and women in a broad social context. She has developed her own self-initiated style of work and relationship. She relates easily to both men and women. At the same time, she is attuned to the limitations of human relationships and recognizes conflict as an inherent component of human life. With humor and imagination, she creates a life context for herself as a person interdependent on others and generative of her own self-esteem.

Dream illustration: The dreamer is working in a women's self-help center where she is actively involved in projects that benefit all women. She feels that her energy is essential to the well-being of the organization.

Someone brings her a gift, a scraggly old pine branch which is presented quite ceremoniously. The dreamer concentrates on the branch, curious as to why it is so precious. She senses that she can move the branch psychokinetically, without touching it. She does this and the branch begins to sway lightly, as in a gentle breeze. The dreamer recognizes that the gift is making things move without mechanically pushing them, without ordinary causality. She notices that she can move any object this way if she chooses. Yet she thinks to herself that this gift has no purpose without some aim. What is gained by arbitrarily moving things through one's psychic powers? Immediately she can sense the potential abuse or corruption of this type of power.

She consults with a physicist about the phenomenon of psychokinesis. He comes to witness her ability. He tells her very solemnly, like a very wise old man, that this is a great gift and that it is called "the organic will." This is a will which stems from consciousness at a submolecular level. The will rearranges or moves the neutrons, protons and electrons into new molecular structures toward a transformation of matter. Hence, what appears to be movement at the level of the phenomenal world is transformation of matter itself through the organic will. She is deeply impressed and wakes up.

Story: unknown
Identity images: Wise Old Man, Wise Old Woman, Androgyne, Compassionate One

As stated previously, these stages of development represent an experiment in clinical thinking rather than an empirically sound paradigm. They were devised in order to provide a map or guide over a wide range of animus images and experiences in women's lives. We have found the scheme to be helpful in distinguishing some basic characteristics about a woman's unexpressed, and perhaps unconscious, assumptions about men and male institutions. We have also found it to be a helpful guide in assessing self-esteem in a woman's relationship to herself. When a woman regards herself from the perspective of the animus, she reveals how much she is able to appreciate and validate in herself.

From the point of view of this book, a central feature of the scheme is its usefulness in discriminating a woman's habitual and fantasied psychological functioning in relationship to her male partner. When a couple enacts the roles of hag and hero, or hag and bully, in the negative mother complex, the woman may or may not be developmentally habituated to the hag position. Success in couple therapy often depends on accurate assessment of the development of each partner. When either one is responding primarily out of the first stage, couple therapy may be contraindicated.

If the woman, for example, is generally oriented to "animus as alien other," she will need various kinds of individual assistance in psychotherapy beyond the couple counseling. In fact, couple work is often not effective if the woman has habituated at the first stage of animus development because the foundation of basic trust in the male partner is not there. At this stage, the relationship with mother or other women is one of dependence and fusion. Even with the help of the therapists, such a woman is often unable to reflect on the metaphorical meaning of her distrust of men and her male partner. A woman in this first stage has not adequately achieved "formal thought operations" (in Piaget's terms) and therefore cannot think effectively about her own thoughts and feelings. She does not have a continuous sense of identity in past, present and future. Such a woman displays a constant inability to distinguish between herself and others in that she "thinks for" others, reads their "thoughts," interrupts repeatedly and is anxiously drawn into other peoples' conversations when they touch on identity concerns of her own.

In terms of her object relations, she has not attained reliable "object constancy" and hence is unable to trust the continuous reliable existence of self and other. Her anxieties concern her self-worth and her compulsive compensations for fears of being worthless.

Often she confuses metaphorical and literal statements in a session. For example, the therapist may indicate that her husband has not really *listened* to what she has said, and the woman responds by saying, "Oh yes, he *heard* me." The client has not understood the difference between the symbolic meaning of listening (which involves empathy in understanding another's perspective) and hearing words. Such a client needs supportive educational work in individual psychotherapy. She needs to acquire social skills and a secure sense of self-worth in being a member of the couple relationship.

A man functioning primarily out of the bully position may display developmental difficulties that indicate he has habituated at a relatively early stage of development. Although we have not developed a scheme of anima development for men, we could use Loevinger's ego development scheme to describe such a man's functioning as "impulsive" or "self-protective."[24] He would have similar problems with object constancy, formal thought operations and low self-worth, although the content of his projections and the affective themes would be different. Typically, the major themes of the habituated bully position concern profound, but hidden, vulnerability and an extreme macho defensiveness. "Impotent rage" is a term easily associated with this type of man, from my experiences in therapy. He is concretely dangerous to his family because of his tendencies toward abuse, aggression and impulsive behavior of all sorts, from alcoholism to theft and other criminal acts.

The therapist, then, must make the decision regarding both the man and woman as to whether the development of the individual has engendered a basic trust in the partner that can be adapted to work on changing the relationship. When partners in a relationship are enacting the negative mother complex, they may appear to be hags and bullies from time to time, especially when they are engaged with each other. If these roles are not habituated attitudes for them, they will be able to function differently with the therapist and to use therapeutic interventions within a couple session to reflect on themselves and change their behaviors. If there are developmental problems, however, they will not be able to shift out of the hag or bully orientation even with the help of the therapist. (This is discussed further in chapter seven.)

When working to change the current dominant conscious attitude, the therapist has to be aware of the resources the client brings to the work. Both the client's individual development and the biases of the culture must be understood in the context of therapeutic goals. In general, the goals of therapy which my co-therapist and I use to guide ourselves in working with couples involve meaning making, empathy and motivation. From a feminist perspective, I am always attentive to the inferior status of female gender identity as it occurs within women and in the society in general, including in men. As a Jungian, I am attentive to the symbolic expressions of human emotions within the intrapsychic and interpersonal fields. These two systems of thought guide us in reaching decisions about goals for therapy and about what kinds of interventions to use.

Individuation as a Developmental Model

The third important contribution of Jung's psychology to psychotherapy is the idea of individuation as the successive integration of unconscious complexes into personal awareness over a lifetime. This contribution is also compatible with feminist therapy because it is founded on an assumption of basic bisexuality or inherent wholeness in the human personality. Jung insisted that the task of individuation in the second "half" of life should be the counterbalancing of the one-sidedness of the first "half" (I use quotation marks here to indicate that the "halves" are not necessarily chronological time periods, but concern the completion of the personality of the individual). Specifically, Jung contended that men had to integrate into their personal identity their repressed feminine aspects, the anima, while women would integrate the animus, their repressed masculine aspects.

Early individuation of the personality, which takes place from infancy to secure adulthood, involves the successive integration of unconscious complexes, "powers out there" in parents (mother and father complexes) and gods (God, king and patriarch complexes), into a personal sense of self. Personal agency, responsibility and identity are the goals of early individuation. A person who has achieved an adequate identity as an adult feels reliable enough, worthwhile enough and useful to others and society. Such a person basically trusts that others, especially the marital partner, have achieved the same status.

An underlying assumption of the theory of individuation in Jung's psychology is that unity in the human personality is never assumed and never entirely achieved. Although unity is a universal striving and a universal potential, the actual state of most people's functioning is a mixture of personal, intentional and rational activities with unconscious complexes or part-personalities which are not fully integrated into consciousness. When working with couples, it is essential to make them aware that they are not simply intentional people. Often their communications, especially when in conflict, are infused with non-rational, unconscious meaning organized around the field of a complex.

While the overall process of individuation in the human lifespan is characterized by a constant striving for unity, coherence and wholeness, on even a moment-to-moment basis people struggle to maintain a continuous sense of being and doing, of personal identity and agency. Over the life cycle, the personality develops by integrating a personal sphere of meaning, with accompanying responsibility, intentionality and self-awareness. When this personal sense of being an adult has been secured, the next developmental task is to relativize personal being. In the second "half" of life, then, the individual develops by recognizing and integrating the meaning of limitation and loss, of inadequacy and fear in self and other. This relativizing of one's earlier adaptation, accomplished through the integration and transcendence of personal loss and the development of an expanded meaning of one's own life, may manifest as a religious orientation, a sense of greater purpose than one's own individual desires or an understanding of human life in a broad social context.

Embracing the hag or confronting the repressed aspects of oneself (often as they are projected onto one's partner) is one way of imaging the first step of individuation in middle and later adulthood. When couples are troubled by the negative mother complex and are relating largely through it, each partner risks a great loss. Together they face the potential loss of their relationship. As individuals, the man stands to lose his wife, his children, his opportunity to be an intimate and valued member of the family, and his relationship to his own inner life. The woman faces the potential loss of the relationship with her husband, the opportunity to revitalize her own female gender identity, and the possibility of becoming a fully autonomous, vital adult. A requirement for further individuation at this point of potential loss is that each person recognize her or his individual task of development. Each person must recognize the need to change in some fundamental way, and that it is not simply the partner or the situation that must change. Recognition of potential loss is often the shock that motivates partners to work on those inner issues which led to stagnation in the relationship.

For both people, embracing the hag involves revaluing the feminine, both inside and outside of themselves. Paradoxical as it may seem, in order for the woman to develop an internal relationship of true partnership with her own repressed masculine, or animus, she must value her own womanliness. Revaluing the feminine entails integrating her own authority and worth by claiming her skills and competence in care-giving and human relationship. For the man, revaluing the feminine typically means claiming his own dependency needs and feelings. Working with couples to embrace the hag usually begins with the shocking confrontation of loss, sometimes provoked (in part) by the therapists. When basic trust has been threatened in the couple relationship, and when resentment, frustration and despair have held sway for some time, people resign themselves to their hopelessness and are not motivated to work on inner issues. When the reality of loss is made conscious through work on the current conscious attitude, the necessary motivation may be regained.

Competing Realities in the Interactional Field

The fourth major contribution of Jung's psychology is the focus on competing, legitimate realities in the interactional field. Jung recognized that communication and expression are governed by competing realities both within the intrapsychic interaction of complexes and within the interpersonal interaction of people. Rational, narrative expression is simply one form of communication or thinking, and not the only legitimate one. Unconscious and non-rational realities do not have to be converted to rational forms in order to be comprehensible. Jung asserted the "intelligence" of unconscious thinking and the necessity of compensating conscious and rational thought with unconscious images. The idea of *collaboration* between conscious and unconscious complexes within the personality, rather than *domination* of the personality by ego-consciousness, is the essence of Jung's psychology. Especially from the perspective of feminism, this idea opens up the world of human communication to legitimate forms of thinking and expression which are non-rational. Images, gestures and emotions are all worthy ways to communicate and can be understood implicitly without having to translate them into rational forms.

Feminist theory has criticized the attempt to impose rational-empirical forms on all human expression. The pressure to conform to the male-dominated sciences has resulted in a subtle form of oppression whereby "making sense" always means being rational, if not empirical. Symbolic, imagistic, gestural and emotional forms of expression are different from, and not reducible to, rational and empirical modes.

Jung's psychology provides a conceptual framework for mapping the interactional field. From Jung and Harry Stack Sullivan I have learned to pay attention to three different competing realities in all forms of human communication. At different times, one or another of these realities will be most useful in making meaning out of expressive phenomena. The following brief descriptions of each reality introduce an expressive form or dimension of interpersonal and intrapersonal reality conceptualized according to Jung's psychology.

Because I will present the complementarity of Jung's and Sullivan's theories more fully in the next chapter, I include here (parenthetically) Sullivan's terms which correspond to the Jungian descriptions. These concepts guide me in working with both couples and individuals, especially in teaching them how to respond to non-rational communications.

Archetype as such (comparable to Sullivan's *prototaxic reality*): basic organizing tendencies or predispositions for expressing human instincts in emotional communication. Since the human "body" is a social group, human instincts bind and separate group members in such a way as to support the survival of the group. Archetypes are expressed as gestures (e.g., smiling, grasping, sucking, etc.), body states (e.g., tension and fatigue) and movements (e.g., rocking, stroking, hovering, etc.). These archetypal expressions, organized around typical human interactions over the life cycle, are imaged in the traditional stories of all cultures and are recorded in myths, religions, literature and art.

Archetypal complex (comparable to Sullivan's *parataxic reality*): integrated collections of images, ideas, actions and feelings organized around archetypes. Complexes can be considered comparable to "affective schemata" or unified thought and action schemes which are habitually enacted around certain meanings such as mother, child and father. Experienced as moods or reactions to stimuli, and in symbolic or ritualistic activities, complexes are infused with meaning. They are motivating in a non-rational way and compel the individual to be or do something. Complexes are imaged in dreams as people or aspects of people, as other dream characters, and as parts of the dream environment. They are non-personal, arising out of universal themes in human society, and are filled with content that is a part of the individual's early and present life context. Complexes are certainly influenced by interactions with other people, but are instinctually charged in ways which are universal among humans. Archetypal complexes are unconscious or partly conscious. They are experienced as invasions of ordinary personal reality and feel familiar only upon reflection. The experience of an archetypal complex is often of an alien character; one feels "beside oneself." Complexes can be interpreted in terms of non-rational, symbolic expression and meaning systems. They can be understood by studying the mythologems of traditional stories and cultural products which are concerned with typical aspects of human living.

Personal-conscious reality or ego complex (comparable to Sullivan's *syntaxic reality*): the center of subjectivity and the tendency to strive for coherence in experience, expressed as "I" and self in a body-image field, feelings and actions. Personal reality develops along the lines of being (identity) and doing (agency). The attributes of being a person are made and internalized as the individual acts in ways which others identify as "personal" (e.g., claiming identity, acting intentionally and being self-aware). This reality is expressed in narrative, historical and rational forms as the "story" of one's life. Although the experience of personal reality is subjective, intentional and rational, its form is also a complex: it is a collection of images, affects, ideas and habitual actions. The personal complex can be considered synonymous with self-identity or ego; calling it "personal" rather than something more abstract, such as ego, helps to place it squarely within the social domain of self-other development as a person. Because this complex is experienced as personal reality and reinforced by the social context of being a person-among-persons, its expression involves a wholly different mode of communication from those archetypal complexes which tend to be less conscious.

The animus is an *archetypal complex* which is the other side of a woman's personal gender identity. As a woman comes to identify herself consciously with certain qualities and aspects of being a person, she excludes others as being "male" or "masculine." These others function as an unconscious complex which is both projected onto others and experienced within the woman. A similar situation exists for a man's conscious identity and the anima complex.

By distinguishing between archetypal and personal reality, it is possible to assist people in claiming what is personal, or within their responsibility, intentionality and identity, and accepting what is archetypal or essentially human. Separation anxiety and fears of engulfment, for example, are feelings associated with the negative mother complex and the archetype of basic attachment (Great Mother); they are not feelings which are under personal control, but are enacted as part of a complex in dealing with another person or with another aspect of oneself. When a complex is differentiated from personal reality, one develops greater freedom to see another person as "ordinary" (rather than as a witch, bitch or hag, for example) and to experience oneself as an ordinary person. Complexes must be understood and acknowledged as inherent in human relating and not the fault of personal reality.

My purpose in this chapter has been to place Jung's psychology in the context of feminism and to show how it can be adapted to a feminist approach to psychotherapy. I have also been defining the terms I will use throughout the book in my discussion of couple relationships. As therapists, we need a unified model for assessing human activities in the framework of meaning, empathy and motivation. Jung's contributions are effective in two important ways. They give us an orientation for working on changing current attitudes toward self and other. They also give us the means for understanding the meaning of non-rational communication both in the moment and in symbolic expressions. As a feminist therapist I advocate a "no blame" orientation in understanding human communications and relationships. When we assist people in becoming more wholly human, we need to be careful not to limit their experience of authority and worth by increasing self-blame or furthering identification with "inferior" qualities. Self-blame and blaming others is so much a part of our thinking about psychological problems that we have to work to stop blaming. My revisions of Jung's concepts of archetype and complex, along the lines that he himself began, can provide a systematic approach through which to assist women and men in accepting one another in an atmosphere of "no blame."

3

C.G. Jung and Harry Stack Sullivan

The two men who will hold a dialogue here have some startling similarities in their personalities and personal histories. They both wrestled with the conflicts of working within and outside the causal-empirical framework of the natural sciences in the nineteenth century. Each man moved substantially beyond those rational-empirical methods which have limited the human sciences until recently. Each theorist was influenced by Freud's method of psychoanalysis. Both of them rejected many of the major tenets of psychoanalysis while retaining the spirit of it as a means for deciphering the non-rational components of human expression. Because Harry Stack Sullivan and Carl Jung have unique individual styles and substantial bodies of work, an imaginary dialogue between them is an effective way to reveal some of their similarities and differences. It will serve principally to introduce Sullivan to the reader who has already encountered a review of relevant Jungian concepts in the preceding chapter.

Before their conversation begins, I want to review some facts and impressions about their lives. Sources for both biography and theory are listed in the bibliography, but are not individually referenced here because of the interruptions such cumbersome notation would create. I have sought to be faithful to the men's styles and meaning in the dialogue I have written.

My purpose in presenting the dialogue is to clarify some of the assumptions I use in treating couples who have problems in basic trust. My own use of Jung's psychology has been broadened and made more practical through my integration of Sullivan's interpersonal theory. Much of my thinking about complex and archetype, about individuation and self, has benefited from including interpersonal relationship as a prominent feature. Because our culture is so overbalanced in the direction of "individualism," we can easily fall into the error of conceiving of the human psyche as an isolated individual when in fact it is always a relational endeavor of "self-other" between persons or complexes.

Carl Jung was thoroughly Swiss in his adaptation and European in his intellectual style. He was steeped in classical studies and was fluent in several modern languages in addition to Latin and Greek. He was oriented toward a philosophical approach to psychology and was minded to pose questions of human meaning in the context of scientific psychology. Harry Stack Sullivan was particularly Ameri-

47

can in his intellectual style and was peculiarly American in the conflicted nature of his personality. He was the product of "not belonging" to an upstate New York rural community in which conformity and puritanism were the rules of the day. His intellectual style was very much influenced by the new American social psychology of the early twentieth century, which involved such contributors as Dewey, Mead and Cooley. Sullivan was interested in a theory of self more from the perspective of experience than philosophy, but his acquaintance with social psychology, anthropology and psychoanalysis compelled him also to look at the broader picture and ask questions of meaning as he examined data.

Both of these men anticipated the work of Jean Piaget in developmental psychology. This is worth noting because Piaget's concept of the "affect-laden scheme" in the "pre-operational thought" of children (prior to logical operations) is compatible with the major concepts for non-rational thought in both Jung and Sullivan. Jung uses the term "complex" and Sullivan uses the term "parataxic distortion" or "parataxic reality." Jung and Sullivan both conceive of personality in terms of its development and share some features of a stage theory of development like Piaget's. Sullivan's model, especially, is a sort of stage theory without a completely formal logic. (A chart at the end of this chapter summarizes Sullivan's stages.) Sullivan's developmental psychology extends vaguely into "adulthood," but it is primarily concerned with infancy, childhood and adolescence. Jung's developmental psychology largely ignores infancy and childhood as it describes the emergence of an "essentially human" personality in middle and later life. Jung was probably the originator of the idea of phases or stages of life which are distinguished by different psychological and social tasks. Keeping the idea of development in the foreground will be helpful in understanding the work of both Jung and Sullivan.

Jung spent his later years, before his death in 1961, immersed in investigations of such obscure subjects as synchronicity (acausal connection through meaning) and alchemy (as a synthesis of opposites in human personality). These preoccupations took Jung substantially beyond the temporal-causal framework of the contemporary scientific psychology. Sullivan spent the latter part of his career, before his death in 1949, attempting to extend the findings and premises of psychology toward the attainment of world peace and an understanding of the non-rational elements of international relations.

Sullivan objected to the application of mechanistic and causal reasoning from the natural sciences to the understanding of human personality. The "private" character of the structural model of ego, superego and id in psychoanalytic theory seemed absurd to Sullivan as a means for understanding the interaction between people. Similarly, he disagreed completely with the idea that the psychoanalyst could ever approach being a "blank screen" for the analysand's projections. Sullivan introduced the concept of the therapist as a "participant observer" engaged in the interactional field of psychotherapy with the client, no matter how little the therapist actually said. Jung had taken an even further step toward the idea of collaboration in the therapeutic encounter when he claimed that in an effective psychoanalysis the analyst was as much in analysis as the analysand.

Certain similarities in the dynamics of Jung's and Sullivan's families might have contributed to the maverick character of the two men's personalities. Each man was the only son of a stalwart, ambitious mother and a more passive, introverted father. Sullivan came from an Irish-American family and grew up as a Catholic in a puritanical Protestant farming community. All of his siblings died in infancy. His mother came from a wealthier and better educated background than his father, who was a farmer. She thought she had married beneath her station and was apparently a chronic complainer and semi-invalid who had a fiery resentment toward her poverty-stricken living situation. Photographs of her in later life give the impression of a solidly strong woman, though crippled by arthritis, who did not give up easily. Sullivan's father, a withdrawn and somewhat insecure man, appears in photographs as a slender, New England-looking farmer. A socialist, he was a self-styled political philosopher who discussed his views at the local general store, where men convened their community meetings around a pot-bellied stove. Sullivan's reports of his childhood on the farm and at school communicate the isolation and painful insecurity felt by the young boy. He felt more related to the livestock on the farm than he did to the people around him, with the exception of one rather sophisticated maternal aunt who occasionally visited the farm. He felt so alienated from his family of origin in early life that he did not speak with the natural Irish brogue of the clan. Later in life, after a serious personality upheaval, he recovered his Irish brogue and lapsed into it on occasions throughout the rest of his life.

Born in 1875, Jung was seventeen years Sullivan's senior. He grew up in an impoverished middle-class family in a rural Swiss canton and was the son of a minister. Jung's mother seemed the more powerful parental figure in that it was she who conveyed to Jung the awareness of a hidden, dramatic personality quite distinct from her ordinary one. Jung had a younger sister who did not achieve much in her adult life; she lived primarily in her brother's shadow until she died prematurely. Jung's father was self-effacing and withdrawn, but apparently quite kind. He provided a model of scholarship for his offspring; he studied classical languages and philosophies which were of little practical use to a country pastor.

Both Jung and Sullivan, then, were isolated children in rural communities. Both men responded as children to their mothers' "unlived lives" and to the influence of strong maternal spirits that yearned for more than the gratifications of their immediate surroundings. Jung was captivated by the "pagan" spirit of the Swiss farmers in his community; he thus felt a deep human kinship that Sullivan was unable to achieve in his childhood.

Each man experienced a wrenching personality reorganization which became the focal point of his psychology. For Sullivan, it was an adolescent crisis which occurred around the age of nineteen (which he described as schizophrenia) and resulted in a partial retrieval of the developmental losses of his earlier life. Sullivan focused much of his theory on the problem of developing a "chum" in pre-adolescence. Relationship with a chum could give a developing individual the means for recovering from earlier parental relationships and could provide a way to practice intimacy with an equal. Intimacy and "consensual validation" with a friend in adolescence were major contributors to psychological health in adulthood, Sullivan contended. Jung's disturbance in personality occurred initially when Jung was about thirty-six years old, after he separated from Freud, the intellectual mentor who had provided the fathering influence Jung had longed for in childhood. Jung devoted much of his subsequent career to understanding personality reorganization in middle and later life, and to the process of integration in the adult personality. The identity crisis of adolescence (most severely expressed in a schizophrenic episode) and the identity crisis of middle life came to be the special features of these two men's developmental theories of personality.

Both men were psychiatrists. Jung received his university and medical education at highly reputable institutions and was an accomplished young scholar by the time he began his psychiatric residency. Sullivan received his education, after he was dismissed from Cornell University (both for academic failure and for "tampering with the U.S. Postal Service"), in the American Midwest in relatively less sophisticated, and certainly less scholarly, institutions. He became a widely read, self-styled scholar in his adult life and was reluctant to admit the "secret" of his earlier education.

Both men did their psychiatric residencies and began their psychiatric careers working in public hospitals with psychotic patients. This, to my mind, is the central most important difference between them and Freud: both Jung and Sullivan learned to "live with" psychotic patients and to appreciate and understand their realities. Jung's idea of the "wounded healer" as the most effective psychotherapist was lived out by Sullivan, who believed that he understood schizophrenic thought processes because he had himself experienced them. In Sullivan's experimental ward for schizophrenic adolescent males at Sheppard-Pratt Hospital in Baltimore, he insisted on excluding most fully trained medical personnel from treating the patients; instead, he chose his assistants from those people he perceived to have had schizophrenic experiences themselves. A modern Sullivanian, Harold Searles, makes an eloquent statement about therapy with schizophrenics, describing what Jung has called the "kinship libido" from therapist to patient:

> The therapist experiences not only the . . . sense of wholehearted commitment to the therapeutic relationship, at a depth which, he now realizes . . . he never felt before; he responds to the patient, during the therapeutic session, as being of boundless personal importance to him, and becomes progressively unafraid to acknowledge this on occasions when the patient needs such acknowledgement. It is not too much to say that the therapist feels the patient as necessary, even, to complete himself; temporarily and acknowledgedly, that is, he feels towards the patient that which the "schizophrenogenic mother" was not strong enough either to acknowledge or to relinquish: the need for the patient to complete her own personality.[1]

Jung, like Sullivan, insisted on recognizing and differentiating the genuine collaboration of the therapeutic relationship, beyond whatever projective and repetitive distortions the client would bring as "transference." Sullivan and Jung focused their therapeutic methodologies and theoretical concerns on what was "genuinely" and "essentially" human in personality and therapy, rather than on "distortion," "repetition" and "resistance." They certainly recognized and named distortions and found therapeutic uses for them, but they did not make the distorted or disguised aspects of psyche the major focus of their work.

Jung and Sullivan were much influenced by modern biology, ethology and anthropology in devising interpretive systems for unconscious or symbolic thought processes. Neither of these men believed that unconscious thought processes could be reduced to rational sentences or that they could be completely understood in terms of disguised wishes and infantile impulses. Rather, they attempted to describe symbolic and gestural communications as simply different forms of human expression, quite distinct from rational syntactical meaning. Both men were concerned with transcending the effects of philosophical dualism and Cartesian dichotomies in interpreting unconscious thought processes.

Even the dichotomy between mental health and mental illness came under scrutiny by both Sullivan and Jung because they recognized the normal disunity of the human personality. The dichotomies of love-hate, aggression-submission, good-bad, right-wrong and doctor-patient were revised by Jung and Sullivan through their interpretations of the full range of human personality. Jung came to believe that the collaboration of conscious and unconscious thinking was the goal of personality development, rather than the domination of the personality by rational thinking. Sullivan believed that human relationship involved competing and co-existing realities which are irreducible and must be fully understood in every human encounter.

An example from Sullivan's psychology of his insistence on the irreducible nature of competing realities or meanings is his revision of the prevalent psychiatric idea that schizophrenic people fear closeness and are detached and hostile. Sullivan asserted that schizophrenic people express their need for contact and love *through* hostile means, which are the only means available to them for "reaching out." In other words, apparently hostile expressions, such as hitting or spitting, have to be understood as reaching out for contact, a meaning opposite to that usually understood by such expressions. Contemporary Sullivanian therapists speak about "malevolent laughter" and "hostile sympathy" in understanding symbolic emotional reality. At the level of emotional and symbolic expression, we cannot "sort out" reality through our typical meaning attributions.

Both men asserted that we are all more "simply human" than otherwise and can intuit or understand each other in immediately accurate ways. The idea that schizophrenic people think or behave in ways which are entirely alien to other people constitutes a decision not to understand non-rational expressions. Both Jung and Sullivan would contend that we all can understand the emotional intent (though not the fantasied meaning) of schizophrenic thought processes through our own experience of emotional reality. We "feel" the rage of malevolent laughter and the warmth of hostile sympathy even when we may deny these feelings rationally.

From Sullivan's point of view, all of human personality is built around relationship and our abilities to constitute "consensual validation" of our experience with another person. From Jung's perspective, a major part of human personality (i.e., the expression of archetypal forms through gesture and image) is universal and archaic. Jung's focus on understanding the meaning of archaic symbolic expressions tends to be intrapsychic or introspective. Sullivan's focus is interpersonal as he seeks to understand what is essentially human and enduring in personality. Whether the focus be on the intrapsychic or the interpersonal, the interest, for each theorist, is in the essentially human, universal and enduring elements of personality. Let us now hear "directly" from the two men in a dialogue about their similarities and differences.

Interpersonal Meets Intrapsychic: A Comparative Dialogue

Sullivan: I would like to begin, Dr. Jung, on a common ground and set a pathway for examining similarities in our theories, with the purpose of informing ourselves and our readers about some of our assumptions in practicing psychotherapy. An area of substantial agreement between us is the idea of "finalism" in your explanation of the meaning of psychic events. This idea you developed in your essay on psychic energy, and it stands in contradistinction to the psychoanalytic theory of libido as a lustful force or drive. If I understand you correctly, you would describe the meaning of psychological events in terms of their purpose after the fact, so to speak. Empirical psychology has been preoccupied with the discovery of causal relationships in a most naive way, it seems to me. In theory and in practice, psychoanalysis has been devoted to the goal of uncovering the "true cause" or force behind a manifest event. Since 1924, when I wrote about some of my initial ideas concerning schizophrenia, I have argued that we must first and foremost assume that a patient's actions are purposive and must look for the meaning in them. If there is one fundamental concept in all of my work it is that things mental are ultimately purposive and must be understood in terms of their final purpose rather than in terms of some arbitrarily selected cause.

I think you and I have hit upon a similar approach here, but I would like to clarify one component of your explanation of psychic energy as finalistic. You distinguish your approach from a teleological theory of psychic energy. I would very much like you to trace the distinction between finalism and teleology, because I think it would put us on the right track for examining the way we treat meaning and symbols in human experience.

Jung: I have avoided the term "teleological" because it is associated with Alfred Adler's psychology, and I think there is an essential misunderstanding in Adler's reasoning about a fictional goal or aim as an explanation of human motivation. Adler's ideas, and most teleological reasoning about motivation, imply that the goal or anticipated end of action is somehow contained in the development of the action, *in potentia,* from the outset. For example, Adler suggests that neurotic fantasies are aimed toward a particular triumph or control which pulls them forward, so to speak. I disagree. My concept of finalism is an explanatory concept for a meaning which can be known only after the fact. We can only look back over a series of events and hypothetically conclude a meaning through our observation of the process. Thus, my conception of psychic energy is not that of a force which pushes or pulls events in the human mind; psychic energy is an abstraction—a hypothetical X—which serves as a means for explaining the purpose or meaning after an event has occurred.

Psychic energy is a construct which has been abstracted by observers in examining the themes and patterns of meaning in human life over time. I have been most interested, of course, in those events in human life which seem to be mere coincidences—things which just "happen" to follow one another. Freud, Adler and you, among others, have also been intrigued by the meaning of what at first appeared only coincidental: a slip of the tongue, a dream image, a joke. In a dream, for instance, we may take the events to be absurd, the mere aftereffects of a stomach upset before sleep. But when we look at the dream in the context of other dreams by the same person over a period of time, we can discover what looks like an aim or pattern in the dream, and the way in which a particular dream fits into the behaviors and desires of the dreamer.

Psychic energy, as a principle for understanding human motivation, is based on the assumption that human behavior is purposive when examined in the context of a human life. One posits the idea of an "energy" to explain the relations of one mental event to another, but the concept of energy itself is subjective and probably the product of the scientific *Weltanschauung* in which we live.

You have postulated a concept of psychic energy based on anxiety as a prime motivation. My understanding is that you see a distinction between anxiety as a sort of energy of disintegration and some other energy as integrating. Could you elaborate on this distinction? I am especially interested in a comparison of my concept of the shadow with your idea of anxiety and security operations.

Sullivan: Yes. To begin, your idea of the shadow seems more compatible with what I have singled out as the most effective security operation, "selective inattention." Your idea of a persona, a mask constructed for purposes of one's social role, is perhaps more similar to my idea of security operations in the "self-system." First, let me elaborate the idea of anxiety as it concerns motivation and security operations. In order to do this, I must enter into what will necessarily be a lengthy discussion of the assumptions of my theory of human personality and the difficulties of living. Before I do so, is there anything else that you would like me to respond to?

Jung: Something I would like to note is the difference in our language and in the images we use to describe psyche. Although we have studied some similar processes of the human mind, we have chosen to describe them quite differently, and I would like to return to this difference after you have explained the idea of anxiety as it relates to your overall theory.

Sullivan: I must begin with a basic premise of my interpersonal psychology which I have called the "one-genus postulate" and which may correspond to your idea of a collective psyche. Here is the postulate: We shall assume that everyone is much more simply human than otherwise, and that anomalous interpersonal situations, insofar as they do not arise from differences in language or custom, are a function of differences in the relative maturity of the persons concerned. With this as a basic postulate, I have insisted that we as psychotherapists can understand even the most eccentric or seemingly unwitting expressions of the most apparently disturbed human beings. You probably know that I describe human personality as the relatively enduring interpersonal patterns or situations which characterize a human life. These interpersonal patterns characterize the development or relative maturity of a human being and are expressed in typical modes of communication. From my clinical observations, I have differentiated three modes of communication or reality that characterize interpersonal experience. You will see that they correspond vaguely to periods of early development and may be more or less securely achieved by any adult.

First there is the *prototaxic mode.* This mode precedes symbolic communications and is expressed and experienced through sentient and kinesthetic activity. Laughing, sucking, grasping, rocking, sneezing and sighing are examples of expressions in the prototaxic mode. Communication in this mode originates prior to the infant's ability to discriminate consistently meaningful visual and auditory images in the environment.

The second reality is expressed in the *parataxic mode,* which is characterized by images or symbols. This mode is expressed and experienced through images which are idiosyncratic, used in ways which are not commonly shared or understood. The symbols refer more directly to each other, such as the "good breast" and the "bad breast" or the "anxious mother" (experienced as the dry breast, for example) and the "good mother" (experienced as the full breast) than they do to a shared reality. As images and symbols, these expressions do not have direct correlates with the experience of other people. The parataxic mode is another preverbal mode of communication, one in which the undifferentiated wholeness of experience is broken down into *gestalts*. Most parataxic imagery is originally connected to felt comfort and discomfort and to their anticipation. We could consider these images to be affect-laden "preconcepts" when they originally occur. They are produced by all of us in dreaming, imagining and creative expression.

The third form of reality is more familiar to us. I call it the *syntaxic mode* because it is expressed and experienced through symbols and images which are shared or have common references. Most of our syntaxic reality is consensually validated through exchange and agreement among people. This type of symbolic expression involves an appeal to principles which are accepted as true or given by the other person or persons with whom one is communicating. In childhood, syntaxic communication begins with the shared and consistent use of language and symbols. Consensual validation is also the means by which we distinguish a continuous sense of self in communication with others.

Thought is organismic activity which is evidenced in the functioning of symbolic expressions that are abstractions from material life events. Symbols of the lowest order are not much abstracted at all. They are of the prototaxic or sentient type and include all of the gestural and kinesthetic expressions which are common to human beings everywhere. Expressions of face, hands and feet occur as the primary modes of communication both in infancy and in the most disintegrated forms of schizophrenia. They are not precisely deciphered or understood outside of the infant-mother pair. In all adult communication, however, they continue to express basic emotional needs and states.

The alternation of need and satisfaction gives rise to the prototaxic mode. The felt comfort of satiation is distinguished from the felt discomfort of tension. Increasingly clear foresight, or anticipation of relief through appropriate action, arises from the experience of this alternation between tension and satiation. The infant's need is expressed in crying, grasping, sucking and the like, and the mothering one responds with tenderness and care. A basic human need or universal dynamism is the need for tenderness. The complementary need in the mothering one is to manifest appropriate satisfaction, or to give tenderness.

The tension produced by anxiety in the mothering one can interfere with the integration of the need-tenderness dynamism between the infant and the responsive adult. Anxiety is a purely disintegrating tension, without any expectable goal or clear means for relief. Anxiety arises in the self-system of the mothering one under threat to her or his self-esteem. Whenever the mothering one, who could be an older sibling or a mother or father, experiences the tension of anxiety, it is communicated as a disruption in the basic dynamism of need-tenderness in the infant-parent pair. When the infant experiences the tension of anxiety, as in the case of the dry breast (which appears to be the good breast but does not satisfy the hunger need), the infant experiences a tension which is different from that of other needs. The tension of anxiety is different due to the absence of anything specific about it. No action of the infant, especially not crying, will consistently work to relieve this tension. As anxiety increases in the infant, it also increases in the mothering one, and nothing works perfectly well to re-establish the tenderness between them.

Now, if the anxiety of the infant and the mothering one become especially acute and the infant's crying is particularly violent, anxiety can actually interfere with respiration and thus produce an infantile fear that becomes terror. Only detachment in sleep can resolve such mounting anxiety. If this type of acute anxiety disrupts the need for tenderness too often, the infant will learn to protect itself through generalized apathy and detachment, as in infantile schizophrenia.

In adulthood, communication through a manner of experience or action, such as falling asleep, is prototaxic communication. Both in times of fatigue and anxiety in normal people, and in psychotic episodes in paranoid and hebephrenic schizophrenics, we see evidence of prototaxic communication. Perhaps the most complex and undifferentiated form of prototaxic expression in adult schizophrenia is laughter. The hebephrenic patient, the most severely regressed of all schizophrenic patients, shows laughter as a characteristic symptom. Such laughter can communicate scorn, hatred, despair, fear and rage in a form so unlike words as to seem completely foreign to those therapists who listen only to language.

The tension of anxiety works, then, to disintegrate or interrupt basic dynamisms that create continuity in interpersonal experience. The tension of need, such as the need for tenderness or food, has an integrating effect on the development of basic dynamisms of human relationship. I want to emphasize the singular importance of the tension of hunger. The integration of hunger toward satisfaction provides a sustaining tension which results in expressions of need in the infant and responses of tenderness in the mothering one. The continuing connection between need and human tenderness is the basis of foresight and language.

Needless to say, the connection between hunger, human relationship, food, and parataxic symbolizations is terrifically complex and not very well understood. If the infant has continuing experiences of distinction between felt comfort and felt discomfort, accompanied by increasingly clear foresight about appropriate actions toward satisfaction, eventually the infant will elaborate a *personification,* or personal image, of the sound, visual, kinesthetic and olfactory representations of the tender mothering one. Similarly, the infant will elaborate a personification of the bad, anxious or terrible mothering one. These personifications contain, as it were, all the collected elements of the infant's experience of the mothering ones who provided care and are not the elaboration of a single person. The infant does not personify *the mother,* but rather makes a collection of felt experiences in an affect-laden construction of "good mother" and "bad mother."

Jung: May I interrupt? Clearly, we both recognize that the devouring Terrible Mother and the nurturant Great Mother are not an individual. Mother, as an image or ideal, is far more powerful and moving than any ordinary person can be. The mother symbol points to a fantastic background which eludes ordinary conceptual formulation. This is an image of an underlying psychic reality which is so inconceivably fundamental and archaic that it can be grasped only at the farthest reaches of intuition and then only dimly.

What you call the personification of the mothering one, I refer to as an archetypal image. My concept extends to the instinctual tendency to form an image of mother as well as the actual experiences of mothering the infant has. There is a symbolic correspondence among all images of mother everywhere that is evidence of the archetypal nature of the image; she is imaged as womb, tomb, vegetation and earth itself, among other elementary forms. I cannot conceive of the symbol of mother or Great Mother arising only from individual experiences. Do we disagree on the origin of the symbol?

Sullivan: Not entirely, but I am curious as to whether or not we need a whole philosophy of symbolic forms in order to decipher the context of meaning in human relationship. Are we better served by elaborate concepts which extend beyond the life context of the person, or by astute and careful observation of the interpersonal field and by the development of a systematic vocabulary for depicting those observations?

Jung: My clinical work with patients in the second half of life led inexorably toward the great traditional philosophical and religious systems of major world cultures. Although I had no intention of straying beyond the confines of medical psychology, I found myself compelled to search among world religions and obscure philosophies in order to decipher the meaning of the images brought to me by my patients. Let me save this point until you have finished your discourse on your personality theory, however.

Sullivan: No doubt we will return to this divergence of our ideas. In any case, it is wholly clear that parataxic symbols are different from words. Words have discrete references and meanings. Parataxic images are difficult to understand because they are a mixture of the individual and the universal, of the literal and the figurative.

The "parataxic distortion" of the therapeutic relationship should be the single most serious concern of the therapist. Lack of adequate discrimination of self, environment and other in the parataxic mode gives this sort of thinking an "overdetermination" of meaning. Words that would normally indicate concrete sense perceptions—such as "in here" and "out there"—take on idiosyncratic and symbolic meaning that must be unraveled in order to understand a patient's intent. A comment like "this room looks so empty" may or may not refer to the environment of the room; it may be an emotional statement about an interpersonal "space" perceived as devoid of tenderness. Needless to say, the unraveling of parataxic distortions requires both an intimate acquaintance with the patient and a lengthy study of this form of communication.

In the normal development of parataxic personifications, the infant discriminates a body-self through "good-me" and "bad-me" personifications. Pleasure from need dynamisms and from hands on genitals and thumb-sucking all contribute to personifications of good-me. Bad-me is personified out of the experience of dissatisfaction due to frustrations of need, rough handling and absent or neglectful mothering. If the experience of anxiety is serious and frequent, either through severe and abusive handling by an anxious parent or through excessive frustration of needs, then a "not-me" can occur as a sort of "hole" punched out of the experience of a body. Severe anxiety inflicted by hostile interactions can result in something like a complete impingement on consciousness, like a severe blow to the head. Not-me experiences can be repeated in adult schizophrenia when emotions are experienced as distinctly concrete attacks or "blows" to a patient's physical body.

If reasonable care has been given, an infant gradually develops a self-system of personifications which contribute to foresight and to the avoidance of frustration. The self-system is a collection of expectations and images called into being in order to avoid frustration and anxiety. It is made up of what I have called security operations or modes for channeling needs and attention. As the self-system evolves toward syntaxic reality and shared communication, these security operations consist largely of habitual defenses against anxiety. Doing things and seeing and hearing things in particularly habitual ways protect the self-system against the anxiety of impingements. Selective inattention is a case in point: a person can both select certain elements out of a collection of stimuli and be inattentive to the selection. For example, I may stare at a flowery pattern on the wallpaper and not see the torn paper at all. Selective inattention protects the self-system against cues, especially in the interpersonal environment, that would produce anxiety. It seems to me that selective inattention results in what you have called the shadow complex. Perceptual phenomena which are subliminally attended to and then blocked out of awareness are "known" at some level of awareness or they would not be selectively blocked. If certain phenomena are repeatedly blocked out of interpersonal awareness, they may well collect around bad-me personifications and limit personal responses.

The one last development of personality that I want to mention here is the development of language as a shared symbolic system. This process originates in infancy, anywhere from nine months to two years. In the syntaxic mode of communication, one has available a repertoire of shared symbols through which one can express feelings, images and ideas. Communication is effective only when it is shared or consensually validated as meaningful by another person. Consensual validation is the foundation of human sanity in that it is the means by which we know the truthfulness of our experience and by which we replenish our self-esteem. Validation of syntaxic expressions becomes the avenue for the development of personal worth and for the further integration of personality beyond basic need dynamisms. Consensual validation within a relationship of intimacy with one's biologically ordained mate is, to my way of thinking, the hallmark of emotional maturity. As you can see, what you have called the archetype of the Self, or the tendency to unity in the personality, I have reasoned from the perspective of adequate and sustaining human relationship. The continuity of being human and the experiencing of oneself as a reliable personal actor depend on consensual validation of worth and the need dynamism of tenderness.

I have gone on at great length here, and I am now quite interested to hear your comments.

Jung: The predisposition for integrating an experience of "self" toward a continuing subjective consciousness or "I" is what I have called the archetype of the Self. In the first period of life, which you have traced out in so much helpful detail, there occurs separation and differentiation of the parental complexes from the ego-complex. What are first established as experiences of "I" and "not-I" arise out of an initial unity. Once a secure and enduring sense of "I" is achieved, there occurs a process of re-integration of the complexes which have differentiated out of the initial unity or wholeness. My own clinical work has been specialized in the period of development that occurs after an enduring intimate adult relationship has been achieved, that is, after adequate ego functioning has been established.

I want to move forward to the problem of *individuation* in middle and later adulthood in order to return to the topic we had earlier touched on, my reasons for establishing a philosophical psychology or a broad-based system for understanding symbolic language from many cultures. I think you were questioning what we might call my metaphysical or metapsychological reasoning about symbols. My clinical work with neurotic and psychotic patients, as well as my own analysis and investigations of dreams, have all pointed to the conclusion that myth is the primordial language of symbolic expression. Common to individual expressions in dreams and symptoms, and to naive cultural products such as primitive art, are certain motifs or patterns of symbols. Careful study of these motifs in their original forms in myths, rituals, art and religion has produced a rich understanding that cannot be encapsulated in abstract concepts. To work with the symbolic expressions of the human psyche one needs broad knowledge of the forms of typical mythologems or symbolic motifs. Image is the language of psyche. Syntactical meaning is the expression of consciousness, which is only one level of psyche.

In my work with patients in later life who are confronting the depression of loss and the despair of meaninglessness, I have found that the richness of imagery is necessary for adequate re-integrations of complexes which have been excluded from consciousness through your so-called security operations. These complexes are, of course, the excluded aspects of personal identity: the shadow, the animus or anima and the unacknowledged persona. Additionally, some individuals are confronting other complexes, such as the negative mother complex, which must be made intelligible and integrated into consciousness. When working with the process of reintegrating or re-uniting "I" and "not-I," in later life especially, mythological images and their shades of meaning are the most effective vehicles.

In nature, opposites seek one another; extremes are always touching. So it is in the unconscious. Words, as discrete references, are inadequate for describing or encompassing symbolic meanings, which are universal. Images in the context of myths or stories help us to discover related meanings which illuminate or "amplify" the image presented by a patient.

I believe that the goal of psychotherapy, and of human development in general, is wholeness. This re-integration process, or the claiming of one's own unconscious complexes, ultimately leads one to religious and philosophical questions. Now I would be only too delighted to leave to the theologian this anything but easy task of understanding images of the Self, were it not for the fact that many of my patients are theologians. They would have hung onto the community of the Church, but they have fallen like dry leaves from that great tree and now find themselves depending on therapeutic treatment. Something in these theologians clings, often with the strength of despair, to the traditional theol ogical explanations, and they appear at my doorway with dreams and waking visions that make them question their sanity. They are seeking firm ground on which to stand, since support from the Church is no longer helpful to them. The process of individuation in later life, like schizo-phrenia, often seems chaotic and interminable at first. Only grad-ually do the signs increase that it is leading anywhere. What is more, the way is never straightforward, but appears to go round in circles. More accurately, perhaps, the process is a sort of spiraling of defi-nite and repeating forms, in dreams and imagination, whose charac-teristic is to define a center.

If you question the necessity of the specifically mythological na-ture of my psychological concepts, I hope I have demonstrated that I sought to be true to the empirical nature of the psyche as I have experienced it in psychotherapy and through my other observations. I have attempted to develop a personality theory which could re-main phenomenologically true to the human experience of psyche. I believe you have aimed for something similar.

Sullivan: You are right, although my arena of observation was more the interactive field of relationship than the imagery of dreams or symptoms per se. Consequently, I have focused my attention on dynamisms and anxiety as motivating "energies" in human develop-ment, whereas you have focused on the concept of a finalistic expla-nation in your construct of psychic energy. I wonder what you find compatible in our systems of thought.

Jung: I suppose that foremost in my mind right now is our emphasis on the archaic or essentially human aspects of personality. We both give much attention to the foundation of basic human functioning as the field out of which consciousness emerges like a speck of light against a vast, dark background. My concept of the archetype, as a basic form for the expression of instinctual needs and responses, seems compatible with the idea of a prototaxic reality. Your descrip-tion of the prototaxic mode is different from Freud's concept of a chaotic, "seething" and undifferentiated id. Prototaxic movements, gestures and expressions, while they are "animal-like," follow partic-ular instinctual forms. I am most interested in your idea of "preconcepts" connected with the parataxic mode. I wonder if you have looked at correspondences in mythologies to the images and expressions you have discovered there. Preconcepts for personifications form a clear parallel to archetypal images which are expressed in psychological complexes and occur in dreams. The complex itself, an affect-laden collection of images, actions and ideas, would seem comparable to a personification—one of a witch or Terrible Mother, for example—that might be feared or experienced in relationship. Parataxic distortions and psychological complexes are clearly non-rational expressions of human meaning that are often implied in an interpersonal encounter as well as experienced intrapsychically. Here again, we both emphasize the predictable, meaningful and formal characteristics of non-rational thought forms.

Your focus on interpersonal relationships as the foundation of psychological development in adulthood seems parallel to my focus on relationship to oneself in individuation in later life. Obviously, neither perspective can stand alone because, in the end, they are one and the same. We cannot establish a true relationship to our fellow man without having realistically engaged ourselves with our own complexes, nor can we confront and understand our complexes in isolation from other human beings.

You and I share a concern to establish a therapeutic relationship which acknowledges the role played by authentic human collaboration. You especially emphasize the role of consensual validation in the therapeutic process and the threat which anxiety presents to the relationship when the therapist is not able to validate the meaning of what the patient presents. As you have heard, I have struggled over the years to consider each clinical case with a freshness of "discovery," setting aside all formal rules in order to engage myself anew with the material presented by each new person. My search to discover the meaning of each new symbol led me to do extensive research into a range of cultures and symbolic systems.

In the end, what I have discovered is something which I think you will agree with: the foundation of the human mind, even in the gravest functional illness, is understandable. The most peculiar behavior and fantasies of the psychotic patient, and the most unusual ritual practices of primitive tribal societies, can all be understood in their deepest meaning because, in general terms, we are all more fundamentally human than otherwise.

*

Although I have put some words into the mouths of these two theorists, I have tried to remain true to their spirits and their work. I constructed the dialogue to acquaint the reader with the ideas I will be using in discussing psychological complexes in the interpersonal field. Because Sullivan's work, especially, may be unfamiliar to the reader, and is not separately considered elsewhere in this book, I will close this chapter with a brief chart summarizing the stages of development traced by Sullivan's personality theory. He indicates that his periods of life are not to be thought of as formal stages because he is uncertain whether they overlap and whether the sequencing is universal. Thinking of his theory in terms of stages is almost inescapable, however, and makes good sense for our purposes. I have included in each stage some of the characteristic features of interpersonal relation.

Sullivan's Stages of Personality Development

(Each column should be considered as additive so that each new achievement includes those which have come before)

Stages	Cognitive and affective self-preoccupations	Concepts of significant others	Patterns of communications
Infancy	good-me, bad-me, not-me (anxiety)	good-mother bad-mother evil mother	crying, babbling, smiling, grasping, sucking (*prototaxic*)
Childhood	my body = myself (beginning self-system)	my mother my father	words, dramatizations, acting-like, sounding-like (*parataxic and syntaxic*)
Juvenile (school years)	myself	compeers (groups)	consensual validation, cooperation, compromise, competition, stereotyping
Pre-adolescence	self-consciousness	chum (one or two friends of same sex)	valuing another as much as oneself, love, loneliness
Adolescence	genital, sexual self	member of opposite sex	security, intimacy, lust
Adulthood	integrated self	all of the above, intimate friends, chums	fully human repertoire of interpersonal relating

4

Enacting the Complex: Hag, Hero and Bully

A couple is enacting the negative mother complex when certain rigid and constraining roles which overpower the individuals are being played out. A complex, you will recall, is an habitual set of actions and feelings enacted within an interpersonal field or, within oneself, as a mood or struggle of inner conflict. When a negative complex is repeatedly played out in a relationship, it can sap the relationship of its vitality and freshness. The negative mother complex is organized around the archetype of the Terrible Mother, the overwhelming and suffocating aspects of attachment and nurturance. When this complex is enacted in a couple relationship, the typical roles taken by the individuals are hag, hero or bully. In our story of Sir Gawain and the Lady Ragnell, these were the roles of Ragnell, Gawain-Arthur and Sir Gromer.

In the interpersonal arena, the hag is on one side and the hero or the bully is on the other. The people involved in the complex feel lost or frustrated, beside themselves for lack of understanding what is going on. I have often heard a man say, with a tone of dismay approaching hopelessness, "I really don't know *what* she wants," when he is heroically confronting the hag in his wife. Although any of the roles of the complex can be taken by either member of the couple, the roles tend to be sex-typed because of the assignment of certain appropriate behaviors to gender identity in men and women, and because of the typical assumptions about what it means to be male or female in our society. In brief, women tend to be assigned the province of nurturance, feeling and relationship in their sex-typed roles both at home and in the professions (e.g., nursing and social work). Men, on the other hand, are assigned the domain of aggression and separation, exemplified in the psychological distancing which characterizes the style of thinking called "rationality." Since sociocultural tendencies are prominent in individuals, women are more inclined to take the hag role and men to take the hero role in enacting the complex, as we shall see.

The Psychology of a Hag

Let me begin by describing the hag. As I mentioned earlier, she was a familiar figure in fifteenth-century popular stories. She is familiar today but has a different name; she is called a "nag" or a "domi-

65

neering mother"—or, in Jungian circles, an "animus-ridden woman." Obviously, her features are the same as they were in the fifteenth century: she is ugly, demanding, "fat" (either psychologically too big or physically fat), magically powerful and voracious in her appetite for eating up children and men. As the typical and prevalent over-whelming, overinvolved mother of contemporary psychotherapy lit-erature, the hag is fused with her children and resistant to giving up control in the family sphere.

The woman who experiences the negative mother complex and regularly enacts the hag feels bitterly hurt: she believes that she is uglier, meaner and more malicious than an ordinary woman can be. She feels herself "infrahuman" or "subhuman" in her meanness and ugliness, and she may feel suprahuman in her emotional powers. She may have given up separating herself from the hag at all be-cause she believes that no one cares about her.

All of us enact the hag from time to time. She overtakes us when we feel overburdened and undervalued, hurt and misunderstood. Gradually, we convert our hurt into resentment, distance, coldness and despairing resignation. As the hag, we live "out in the woods" and do not feel ourselves to be worthy or legitimate members of our families. While the woods are just the place for a hag, no ordinary person wants to live there alone. Therefore, the isolated aloneness of the hag becomes a great burden which is eventually accompanied by panic. The woman experiences a panic that no one will ever rescue her because her feelings and her responses have become so alien that no one can understand them. To some extent, such a woman gives up on words: she no longer tries very hard to describe what she is experiencing because others have told her—and she herself believes—that she "doesn't make sense." She may offer brief de-scriptions, but most of the time she will simply cover over her feelings with attempts to control, condemn, retaliate against or serve others.

Here is how my co-therapist and I have come to recognize a hag in a contemporary couple or family. The most prominent feature of the hag is her self-hatred. She describes herself as a disaster: she is fat, ugly, stupid and unattractive in the extreme. Yet she also feels too powerful and may be apologetic about this; she may say, for example, "I feel like I am always nagging my kids and making their lives miserable, but I can't seem to stop." She feels at fault for most of the misery in her family, but she does not know why. Often she openly calls herself a "bitch" or "nag" and finds that her partner readily agrees with her, confirming her self-hatred.

The hag-identified woman gave up on her body a long time ago. Overweight is a prominent *personality* feature of all the hags we

have seen in therapy. Whether or not the woman is really overweight, she *feels* fat and, if she is influenced at all by the cultural
standards for slenderness, is self-condemning about her size. Our
current cultural preoccupation with slenderness in women is sympto-
matic of our collective problems with the negative mother complex.
Geneen Roth, who treats women with problems of compulsive eating, says the following about the effect of fat on women's identities:

> Being and/or feeling fat is usually different for men than for women.
> A man can eat compulsively, be overweight, dislike his body and still
> be thought of—and think of himself—as attractive. . . . On the other
> hand, a woman's appearance is crucial to her evaluation as a human
> being; a woman feels she *is* what she looks like. She may be brilliant,
> perceptive and competent, but if she is fat, she has to struggle to
> prove her worth. . . . Whereas I have met many men who like their
> bodies, men who don't even think about their bodies, I have *never*
> met a woman who liked her body without reservation.[1]

A hag-identified woman has usually condemned her body to isolation and will reluctantly "give over" to intimate, sexual encounters
with nagging anxiety about her disgusting appearance. Naturally,
her sexual aloofness is taken as evidence of her "desire to control,"
and she may then be further depreciated by her partner.

Another way my co-therapist and I can recognize the hag—beyond her own self-hatred—is by the way in which she is treated as a
mother or wife in her family. In one kind of family, she is heroically
endured by her Gawain-husband, who repeatedly asks her what it is
she wants, and then promptly fails to understand. Her children and
her husband have learned to tip-toe around her as though she were
about to eat them up. They do not give her direct eye contact; when
she says "look at me," they become reluctant and apprehensive,
acting as though she could suck out their souls. The woman herself
may have learned to avert her eyes, to look down toward the floor
or out the window, sighing very heavily.

She implies by her behavior that no one will understand her. She
is right, no one does—not in her family anyway. This is true partly
because what she says does not "make sense." She does not bother
to construct a logical sequence or to be specific about her feelings,
although she can do so when she is not communicating with family
members. Members of the family, usually the children, will "fill in"
for her and either translate some of her non-verbal meaning into
words or provide distracting behaviors that communicate the mother's feelings of isolation and anger.

While this kind of family heroically endures the hag, in another
type of family the hag is not so well tolerated. In the Gromer type of

family the man *bullies* his wife and children most of the time. He demands their attention, love, involvement and obedience. He is identified with macho ideals and is openly aggressive and frightening with his physical strength or emotional power. Gromer tells his wife that she (and her mother) are "impossible to live with." He keeps the hag out in the woods and then is surprised and dismayed when his son has difficulties with the female authority of teachers at school, when he is a bully on the playground or becomes a "juvenile delinquent," aggressively damaging others' property or assaulting young women. Gromer never comes to therapy on his own; he is always brought into treatment, usually by the acting out of his children, who are unconsciously protecting and rescuing the hag.

In both types of family constellations, there is almost always a particular, prominent feature of the negative mother complex: no one is aroused by the mother's tears. Her tears are met with disdain and anger. After all, as we know from the fifteenth-century psychology of the hag, her tears are not *real tears*. The hag hides behind maliciousness and control; she is "laughing" her hideous, contemptuous laughter when she appears to be crying as a woman. Other family members respond to the non-rational meaning of the complex when they meet the mother's tears with disdain.

I will now present a case of a hag and hero in couple therapy. First I will talk about Louise, who is the unwilling hag in response to her husband Larry's rational heroism. Later we will meet Larry. Louise and Larry are prototypes or caricatures; they are not based on any particular case we have treated in psychotherapy. Louise is an amalgam of the many women my co-therapist and I have treated who have "brought their husbands" into therapy.

Louise as the Hag

Louise presents herself as every bit the "middle-aged woman." She is plump and dressed in drab colors that inhabit her washable, nondescript stretch trousers and simple, button-down blouse. She is slightly nervous in her manner; she sits on the edge of her chair, fingering her hastily combed hair or her glasses. Her face, no longer attended with cosmetics or other artifice, is stiff and set; she speaks without apparent emotion. As she looks at the floor or out the window, she lists grievances about her children, her husband and her boss at work, where she is an executive secretary. Her everyday life sounds like a series of stressful events and duties. She covers any vulnerability to the effects of this stress by her organized manner, and by sarcasm or complaint. She seems to believe that her husband and children "could help out more around the house," but when the therapist asks her about this more specifically she says, "Well, they already help out so much and they complain about doing more." She says this in a defensive manner, as though her family were being attacked by her own grievances.

As the therapy session proceeds, Louise behaves in a confusing way that mingles intrusiveness with aloofness. While she appears to be emotionally distant from any encounter, she often interrupts other people and speaks out whenever her anxiety is aroused by something that is said. The therapist can become irritated with these interruptions and assume that Louise is attempting to control the therapy session with her intrusions. She is overly apologetic when confronted, however, and seems to fault herself doubly for anything the therapist suggests might be her doing in the family's difficulties. She displays a peculiar, compulsive kind of caring for family members, both in her stories of household chores and in her behavior in the session. She tidies up and notes others' needs before they are expressed; for example, she may give someone a tissue or offer to let a young child play outside if the child is getting restless. Louise apparently provides care partly to cover her own nagging doubts that there is no goodness in her love and that she has no personal worth. If she *appears* to be needed, then she may not be "found out" to be worthless.

When asked about her own desires for the therapy, Louise talks only in terms of others' behavior. She insists that Larry never tells her what is on his mind and that she has to drag everything out of him. She seems to want him to be more expressive emotionally and to empathize with her involvement in care-giving. She wants him to help out around the house, but she wants him to do so in the ways that she needs help. She would like Larry to keep his nose out of her business and to be "more of a man." Most of her desires are confusing and contradictory on a rational level, but we get the strong feeling that she wants a partner in Larry, not a father or son.

What has happened to Louise? We discover that Louise was once a rather romantic and energetic woman who believed that family life would suit her. She was very much in love with Larry when she married him twelve years ago and looked forward to their raising a family together. Larry's ambitions to run his own business and his desire to make money suited her very well, and she continues to support his career; she was and is "proud of him."

When we ask more, we find that she has not lost her idealism about Larry. She sees him as an intelligent, capable, and sensitive man who is respected by his children and by the community. When he is functioning publicly, she is especially fond of him and would like some of that warm, competent attention turned toward her and the children. She has lost faith in herself, however, and does not believe that she can attract Larry based on her appearance or her work. She thinks she is ugly. She *knows* she works efficiently and diligently at home; and while she is "not perfect," she does what she can to love and provide for her family. She makes little money at her secretarial job, but there, too, she works very hard. She knows the routine at work and has some good ideas about how to improve office management. Her boss, however, does not seem to want her "bossing him around" and typically ignores her suggestions.

Louise has gradually retreated into self-hatred and despair about her goodness, her worth, her beauty and now, finally, about the validity of her own preferences and perceptions. She is afraid that she is "going crazy."

Social Aspects of the Negative Mother

From my Jungian and feminist theoretical perspective, Louise is caught in a larger socio-cultural problem, the hag problem of the negative mother complex. She feels no personal authority, worth or competence, and these feelings are reinforced by a society that systematically devalues care-giving, both in the professions and at home. Rewards, status and influence are not connected to nurturance of the young or to the human services of care-giving. Even in this period of "women's liberation," individual women continue to bear the major responsibility for nurturance and development of the young. This is actually a relatively new social situation, deriving partly from the influence of psychoanalysis on the rearing of children, and it is an impossible responsibility. In the past, not even the distant past, responsibility for the next generation was at least nominally shared by a group of adults. Women were not burdened with explanations of themselves as the "causes" of psychological problems; they were not called "schizophrenogenic mothers," "domineering mothers," or "suffocating mothers." Even young adults felt the burden of responsibility for their own independence upon entry into adulthood. We now see people in therapy who are in middle (35-50) and later (50-65) life still explaining their problems and struggles in terms of what mother did or did not do for them. Images of the overwhelming and engulfing mother dominate the psychotherapy literature from psychoanalysis to family therapy, and infuse our popular psychology with a "fear of mother" and a "wish for mother" which is archetypal, impersonal and extremely troubling for individual women.

The problem of the hag is not an individual problem and cannot be solved on that level. Despite its individual enactments and the countless stories about women's inaccurate empathy, fusion with their children and compulsive, overcontrolling manners, the negative mother complex is a social problem. On the individual level, we can treat it by helping women to separate their identities from it and to retrieve the sense of being a person having legitimate female authority. We can help women appreciate the energy and power of the hag in themselves, in terms that are positive and supportive of their female identity. We cannot, however, stop the enactments of the complex without a general revaluing of the archetypal concerns of attachment in human relationship.

The broad social problem of our devaluation of the feminine in human life must be addressed. As previously noted, by the "feminine" I mean those activities and feelings concerned with nurturance, attachment, care-giving, emotional expression and other aspects of "ordinary life." These qualities should not be identified with sex-typed roles or with women. So far there is no clear evidence that the gender category "woman" has specific activities and concerns connected to it across cultural and social situations.[2] I prefer to separate the archetype from the woman and to speak about the feminine as an instinctual-emotional response in human beings, one that involves nurturance and sustenance, as well as suffocation and death. The instinctual dimension of attachment-separation, as described and researched by John Bowlby and his colleagues,[3] is comparable to the archetypal feminine in the discussion which follows. The problem of devaluing the feminine has become fused with women's identity, however, because the provinces of care-giving and relationship have been assigned to women. Primary responsibility for the development of the young has been fashioned into a cultural institution called "motherhood" which oppresses women with low pay, low status and a predetermined outcome of "career incompetence." This institution, not the activity of mothering itself, is at the root of our contemporary hag problems.

A woman's identity, from at least late adolescence on through the life cycle, is tied up with motherhood. Whether or not she chooses to mother, she will be questioned, prodded and analyzed about her choice. Whereas there is little public concern about whether or not men choose to father children (there is, in fact, a somewhat popular trend of denying and fleeing paternity), there is a great deal of concern about the woman who does not choose to mother, especially among psychotherapists and analysts. Although a woman's identity is bound up with motherhood, she has no "good" choice regarding the institution. If she decides to mother and to dedicate herself to others' development, she will be financially dependent, she will carry low social status and she will be unprepared for a career at the end of her active involvement in motherhood. If she chooses not to mother, she will be viewed as inadequate in her femininity and perhaps troubled in her identity.

Those women who devote about one-fourth or one-fifth of their actual lives (18-20 years of mothering out of a predicted 78 years of life) solely to the occupation of motherhood are not prepared to re-enter adult life with any belief in their authority, competence or personal worth. The character of female authority which emerges in the overwhelming and irritating mother voice derives directly from the fact that most of us were mothered only by females. Both the outer and the inner "voice of conscience" structuring our daily lives and telling us what to do was a woman's voice. It is this powerful force of female authority from which we separate and differentiate in order to achieve our own identities; that is, we must differentiate the authority of the mother complex from our sense of self (ego complex) in order to become mothers or fathers ourselves. When adult women speak with authority, especially in their roles as mothers in families, they are defended against and felt as "overwhelming" partly because they are the sole providers of intimate care and protection of children. When a woman, in any social context, is insistent, angry or convinced of her authority, she is often interpreted as domineering, overwhelming or overcontrolling. Rarely is she simply understood to be angry or authoritative.

Recall the national survey on sex-role stereotyping in our society, referred to in chapter two. The survey revealed that the stereotyped masculine traits which cluster around "instrumentality" and "competence" are considered more desirable than the stereotyped feminine traits which cluster around "expressiveness" and "dependence." College students and mental health professionals, as well as a broad cross-sectional sample of adults, perceived the ideal woman as less competent than the ideal man, and the healthy mature woman as more submissive and dependent than either healthy men or any "healthy adult." As I pointed out, this highlights the double bind women are in regarding their own authority. If they adopt behaviors specified as desirable for adults, they risk censure for their failure to be feminine. If they adopt behaviors that are designated as feminine, they are necessarily deficient with respect to general standards for adult behavior.

The combination of excluding men from mothering roles and attributing inferior human qualities to female gender constitutes the social problem resulting in the negative mother complex. The complex manifests in a tendency for women and men in couple relationships, especially after basic trust has been secured and then lost (e.g., through betrayal), to engage in the roles of hag, hero and bully. The hag is a negative and controlling authority who intrudes on others, especially dependent others, with her selfish and manipulative schemes. The hero, on the other hand, is a competent, rational authority who "keeps his distance" and is admired for his humane values and good judgment. The hero presents himself as authoritative and self-esteeming.

As I present Larry in the hero role of the negative mother complex, let us remember that in the story both Sir Gawain and King Arthur represent "poles" of heroic enactment: Arthur represents rational authority and Gawain represents youthful and accommodating bravery. In the early part of the story and until the essential denouement, when Ragnell asks to be kissed, Gawain is the naive knight errant who "rushes in where angels fear to tread." The rational Arthur and the courteous Gawain thus portray the heroic qualities that constrain our hero Larry in his embrace of Louise.

Larry as the Hero

Larry is a youthful-looking middle-aged man, slender and somewhat slouching in posture. He is confident in his easy manner, smiles a lot and speaks in a gentle but firm tone. As we see Larry in his corduroy trousers and button-down pastel shirt, the word "pleasant" comes to mind. Although Larry is balding and wears glasses, there is something from boyhood that seems to shine through his countenance, and his unwrinkled face conveys a youthfulness that is vulnerable and, at times, even "weak."

Larry has come to therapy "to help Louise and the kids." Both he and Louise agree that she has been "dreadfully unhappy lately," and neither of them seems to be able to solve "her problem" or even to determine what the problem is. Larry hopes that the therapists can tell him "how to make Louise happy" because he is eager "to settle this whole thing"; he is beginning "to lose patience with Louise's constant complaining." Also, Larry confesses early on that the two of them have been "through this counseling thing before" and that he doesn't believe this "therapy stuff" really works.

Larry is logical and well organized in the stories he presents. He tells us about his work in selling small computers, how he has gradually built a good career for himself and how he encouraged Louise to go back to work when the kids were both in school. (Their children are eight and ten years old; the younger one is a boy.) Larry likes to know "the facts" about any situation, and he wants to know our fees and what we "think is wrong" immediately. We can easily see that Larry is a "good guy"; he is mild mannered and reluctant to really get angry. He leaves confrontation and conflict to others whenever possible and prides himself on being "a family man." He prefers the world of reason to emotions and often says things like "If we could just be rational for a moment..." after Louise expresses her grievances or interrupts the therapists.

Larry seems perturbed and ashamed to be in therapy, however, and is uncomfortable when the therapists get "too personal" with him. He challenges us repeatedly to "find out what Louise really wants" and to get on with our business. We both find Larry easy to follow and experience him initially as much more likable than Louise. His words make sense, but he seems uncomfortable. He refuses to engage in any "babble," but has a curious capacity to set the therapists on edge with his mild challenges of our authority and rationality.

The Hero as a Collective Problem

Larry is similar to many heroic husbands of feminist wives we have seen in therapy. These are Gawain characters, at the wedding banquet or in the bridal chamber prior to Ragnell's challenge. They give lip service to the ideals of equality in partnership with women and to their concern for relationship and care-giving. These are the husbands who "allow" their wives to go back to school and who accommodate to the wives' demands to "do the laundry on Friday evening, watch the kids from 4 until 7 p.m. on Mondays and Wednesdays" and so on. The neighbors watch these Gawain characters attempt to adapt to their wives' "demands" and then sigh and click their tongues (like the courtiers at the wedding banquet), saying, "Poor Mr. Gawain! He does so much for that irritating woman and she is never happy. Look how he is stuck with those kids, night after night, and he earns the living for the family. Besides, she is such a bitch, always complaining about what he doesn't do. She doesn't know how lucky she is to have him. She'll find out when he just gives up one day and leaves her there, with all her bitching and complaining. That's what she really deserves."

Gawain was giving lip service to Arthur when he accepted the challenge of Ragnell without really considering the situation in terms of his relationship to Ragnell. He was willing "to marry the Devil himself" in order to save the king. It was the rational authority and patriarchal power of the king that Gawain was wedding, not Ragnell. Arthur, on the other hand, was not even up to gallantry. He was giving lip service to the ideals of heroic knighthood when he agreed to have his favorite nephew cohabit with a hag. Arthur was trying to save his head and was willing to do almost anything to get out of the confrontation with the ugly bully Gromer. When the time finally came for Gawain's wedding, Arthur wanted to delay or re-arrange the situation because even his nephew's confrontation with the nasty hag was too much for a poor old king. This kind of lip service to equality and humanitarian ideals is familiar. White males are well known for saying, "Of course I support equality for Blacks (or Puerto Ricans or other oppressed minorities), but that doesn't mean I would want my daughter to marry one."

The story of Gawain and Ragnell has a particular focus on "lips" because of its hag heroine. Hags cannot be kissed directly. If Ragnell were really a hag, Gawain would have had his soul sucked out by her on the wedding night. Because Ragnell knows underneath that she is actually a fine and beautiful woman, she is confident of her authority and power. She says to Gawain, "Come and kiss me." She challenges his lip service to ideals and activities which look good but are, in fact, dangerous to his independent heroism. Ragnell, as the oppressed woman, says, in effect, "It is not enough to simply agree to help out around the house, I want you to embrace the household and me, with the full range of your intelligence and feeling."

The story shows us the character of the hero as partner. He cannot fight the hag with the rationality with which he orients himself in collecting data and amassing evidence. Reasonableness and the cold, hard facts are useless in relating to the hag. Nor can the hero bribe the hag with material rewards: jewels, gold, property and money are of no use to her because she has been stripped down to a terrible isolation that can only be reached through a new trust and vulnerability. The very rewards which might have attracted the woman to marriage with the hero in the first place are now useless to her; they are merely the evidence of her error in trusting a man who could not be her real partner. If the hero cannot move beyond rational attempts at problem solving, beyond the material powers of his authority and beyond his dreadful fears of the hag, he will not retrieve the "youthful princess" in his wife. Nor will he be able to save his head and attain a new sense of meaning in his further development as a man.

I would like us to consider the proposition that it is the contract of marriage itself that casts the spell of the negative mother complex. As an institution, marriage was designed for men to possess women as property and to claim their rights of paternity. With Gawain, Arthur is quick to say, "I cannot give you my nephew Gawain—he is his own man"; with women, however, it remains true that they are "given" in marriage by their fathers to their husbands. This passing on of the female as property is a major factor in the undermining of intimate relationship in marriage. No matter how rational the part-ners may be in entering this cultural institution, they will not be able to avoid its unconscious meaning. Whether one rewrites the marriage ceremony, refuses to be given by father to husband, refuses to assume the husband's name (i.e., by keeping the father's name as one's own), or makes countless other rational arrangements (e.g., living together prior to marriage) in an effort to avoid the collective meaning, those efforts will not work. When people engage the institution of marriage in their lives, they engage the negative mother complex because their friends and families, and their children and dreams, will not let them forget the actual meaning of the institution.

Among contemporary men, the transition from the heroic, rational and authoritative posture to partner of Ragnell is an extremely difficult one. Although the husband enters marriage saying, "I want to share the child-rearing and housework, and I will be your equal partner in the affairs of ordinary living," he will find this a difficult and elusive promise to fulfill. Men have not been trained or sensitized to the responsibilities or skills entailed in care-giving. Much skill and competence are involved in preparing meals, in empathic response to others' pain and in coordinating the chores and activities of a household, though most of us do not consciously recognize this. Boys have excluded from their identities the very perceptual priorities and emotional expressiveness that they will need in order to parent and manage with intelligence the concerns of the home. To make matters worse, they have learned repeatedly, on every conscious and unconscious level, that they should not allow a woman to tell them what to do. Untrained, unmotivated and unaware of the real competence of women in care-giving activities, the grown man will feel as if he must refuse the advice and guidance of his wife if he is to retain his "manhood." This is the dark and dangerous situation that therapists confront in couples who have lost basic trust in each other as partners and who refuse to value the feminine in their daily lives.

The culture does not reward or reinforce any motivation a man may have had to share care-giving. What could be the motivation to learn the skills and emotional responses that women know in providing care and protection? What opportunities for income or status open up to men who have mastered these tasks? None, of course. So even the most well-intentioned young heroic husbands usually go "out to work" and leave the arena of home and family, both by separating themselves physically and by further differentiating themselves emotionally.

Speaking rationally, we know that the family wage system is rapidly disappearing and that at least forty percent of married American households have both partners earning a living for the family. How is this explained or managed within the couple relationship? Usually the man earns more money because the kinds of employment he seeks, the skills he has attained and the attributions associated with his gender are all connected with greater material rewards.

The husband who earns more money outside the home typically carries over to his life in the home the awareness of his greater earning capacity. Having agreed to share household duties with his wife, the heroic husband cannot understand (no matter how much he rattles around in "the facts") why his wife is unhappy with his performance since he earns more money than she does *and* carries out his assigned chores at home. Although his housework may exude incompetence and his care of children and partner may have the character of thinly disguised boredom or frustration, he is certainly "doing his part" and has agreed to his wife's "demands." Both partners repeatedly review all of these facts. The husband seems heroic, especially compared to other men they know, and the partners cannot understand why the wife continues to be unhappy. Of course he could not be expected to "take orders" from his wife, or to adopt her style of housekeeping, but he has tried to accommodate to everyone's needs in the "best" way he can.

The only motivation to change, and it must be a motivation to change himself and his real priorities in life, has to come from the hag—or from the bully—at this point. The motivation is non-rational, emotional, intuitive and compelling. It can come from a threat to "chop off his head" or from a confident challenge to his authority by a Ragnell hag who says, "*I* know the answer. Your life is in my hands."

The major problem faced by the Arthur-Gawain heroic husband is one of believing the hag when she presents him with such a challenge. Paradoxically, the heroic husband looks to the hag or the therapist or the wife (or his "other woman") to do what only he can do. Larry asks the therapists to "make things better" and to "tell him what to do." Because Larry believes that Louise and the therapists are inferior to himself, however, he cannot take their advice. In his Arthur stance, Larry wants only "the facts" and simply cannot accept anything but a rational argument. He demands that everyone speak *his* language. "You are not making sense," he says repeatedly to Louise and the therapists when they talk about the importance of a feeling life and empathy. This heroic notion of "making sense" is a refusal to listen to any formulation of meaning that is not rational— or profitable. Consequently, the hero cannot listen to his wife, his children or other people when they are being "crazy" or "overly emotional." He tunes them out, denies their meaning, and argues with the deficits in their reasoning. The willing hero Gawain refuses to be led by a female authority. He will accept the authority of the king in deciding matters of heroism and challenge, but he will not be led by a demanding woman who insists her answers are right.

Moreover, the Gawain hero denies his anger at his haggish wife and tends to resist with a stubborn smile. Occasionally, he gives over to bully enactments and manifests the rage that he has learned to fear. The female authority of the hag, her insistent and angry confrontation, is anathema to the heroic Gawain, and he wants to exclude it from his identity in every way possible. As he does this, he conveys a disgust for this way of being that is clear to anyone around. In the presence of Gawain, no one wants to enact the hag. His wife, when she is identified with the hag, is enraged by his rejection. `

The Bully Role

In the second or third therapy session with Louise and Larry, I confronted Larry directly and angrily about his refusal to look at the implications of the way he had abandoned his wife at home with her chores and children. I did so in regard to a particular task we had asked him to do after the previous session. Larry became infuriated, telling me that I didn't know what I was doing and that everything I had suggested was "worthless" and that my ideas were "obvious"— that is, he had thought of them all himself and knew they would not work. Besides, he believed that I was "churning up" his wife and "making things worse." He thought I was "probably just an angry woman" and wondered why my own marriage "hadn't worked" (he knew I was divorced by the different names on my diplomas hung on the office wall, a common way in which a woman displays her private life publicly as a result of the institution of marriage).

Larry had become the bully, so I could finally face him with the extent of his own anger at his wife. We will find out more about assisting Larry later. I have used the above example as a means for introducing the bully role in the negative mother complex. Most of the time, the man may be secure in an heroic, rational position, but when something "too much" happens (often as a result of the claiming of authority by an "inferior," often a woman), he will lose his heroic posture and act as if his head had been chopped off. In the marital couple, the hag and the bully will fight and feathers will fly, but nothing is resolved although tension may be relieved temporarily. Basic trust is threatened when the hag and the bully fight.

The bully role is characterized by a macho attitude and an open hatred of the feminine, whether in men or women. The bully is hostile toward psychotherapy, feelings, the women's movement and anything which smacks of "weakness" in a man. Actually, the bully represents an extreme interpersonal position which usually is a temporary state in any individual. Although such a man may experience some social support for his attitudes of aggression against women, he feels very alienated from others and from feelings of goodness in himself. Similar to the hag, the bully-identified man is self-contemptuous. He has stopped really trusting others to care about him and has built up a protective screen of aggressive and hateful prejudices to stand in the place of vulnerability to others. At the foundation of his scare tactics is enormous fear, both of others' potential hostilities and of his own rage. The bully-identified man is the rapist, the wife abuser, the child beater who is so blindly afraid that he can only direct his fear into an attack. The television character Archie Bunker is a humorous prototype of the less harmful bully. Because Caroll O'Connor is such a fine actor, we can often sense the vulnerability of Bunker just under the surface; he shows the childish fear of an "abandoned boy."

In the story of Gawain and Ragnell, the bully is imaged by the initial interaction of King Arthur and Sir Gromer. On the conscious side, the bully-identified man acts like King Arthur did initially: he attempts to possess what is not his, and then does not acknowledge his debt. Arthur is out hunting in woods which are not his, and he makes a kill that he would blithely claim as rightfully his.

The medieval condition of the marriage contract is parallel to the action here. The woman becomes the man's possession, and he has property rights to the children who bear his name. He attempts to possess what he cannot own, someone else's freedom. The irony of the institution of marriage, the legal-social contract entailing a lifelong pledge of the wife to the husband (this is still the current form, pronouncing the couple *man* and wife), is that the contract was created by patriarchal Church Fathers of the fourth and fifth centuries who were celibate themselves and condemned even the sexual intimacy of marriage. The special mixture of spiritual union and property rights in marriage emerged for the first time in Western society around the time when the emperor Constantine inaugurated an alliance between the Church and the State. Up until that time, liberal Roman divorce laws had prevented the marriage contract from binding individuals over a lifetime.

In *Life After Marriage*, A. Alvarez argues that the constraining form of our contemporary marital contract can be traced back to the early Christian Fathers, "whose hysterical intolerance of the flesh" led to a unique situation in the history of marriage in Western

try the old testament

culture, that is, a lifelong, legally binding contract developed as punishment for fornication. Alvarez writes:

> The borderline between chastity and satyromania, between sanctity and farce, was shadowy but impossible to recognize at the time. And because this perverted, unnatural lust for sexual purity was a qualification for sainthood, it produced a permanent deformation in European morality, splitting body from soul and goodness from desire, changing marriage from a blessing into a grudging concession which would spare those incapable of holy chastity from the sin of fornication, and surfacing in the belief . . . that true passion is always doomed and tragic. On a more practical level, the Canon Law which dominated Europe for fifteen hundred years was built specifically on this psychotic no-man's-land.[4]

The zealot's disregard for basic human feelings, combined with the legal possession of wife and children, characterized the context of contractual marriage when it came into being in the Middle Ages.

The combination of emotionality and legality reflected in the institution of marriage itself emerges in the interchange between Arthur and Gromer near the beginning of our story. Arthur represents the State and its concern for property rights; so does Gromer. Arthur intrudes unknowingly on another's territory and attempts blithely to claim the kill that is not rightfully his. Gromer intrudes forcefully to "act out" his own aggression. (In some versions of the story, apparently Arthur actually gave some of Gromer's land to Gawain; in other versions, the cause for Gromer's rage is less clear although it appears to concern property rights.) The fusion of Arthur-Gromer displays the typical bully role.

On the more conscious side, at least from the point of view of appearances, the apparent hero enacting the bully role is "just being reasonable" when he chastises his wife for "not doing her part." He may say, "I earn the living for the family. Her work wouldn't pay the gas bill, and she expects me to do the dishes? That's women's work. Why do you think I got married?" He argues from the position that money and property speak louder than equality or human feelings. This is a common attitude in our society, and many people would endorse its "sound common sense." On the other hand, if someone (especially a woman) steps too far into his domain of property-as-freedom, he flies into a rage. In his enactment of Gromer the bully, he "chops off the head" of Arthur, in the sense that his reasonable side disappears. Now he just gets out his physically threatening weapons, or their emotional counterparts (angry threats), and wants to fight. If the therapist can arouse a more heroic and courageous response in such a man playing out the bully role, then it is clear that he is only temporarily identified with the complex. If, on the other hand, the man regularly fluctuates between a "rational" intolerance for human feelings and rageful threats, it is very likely that he is identified with the bully in a deeper and more permanent way.

Like the woman who has not developed beyond the early stage of animus development, such a man needs much additional therapy to progress in his own development. We have found that "hard-core" bullies are difficult to reach in psychotherapy because they are "in the woods" themselves—they are alienated due to lack of basic trust.

The Negative Mother Complex

This chapter has presented the roles of hag, hero and bully as parts of a fairly detailed map of the interpersonal space or interactive field of the negative mother complex. I have used the story of Sir Gawain and the Lady Ragnell to illustrate how Jung's psychology can help us understand non-rational communications between people. Each of the roles illustrated in the story can be enacted by an individual outside of an intimate relationship. I believe, however, that these identity roles must be continually reinforced within an interpersonal field in order to be sustained as ongoing, non-rational orientations. Everyone experiences some identification with the hag when feeling hurt, resentful and powerless to do anything about these feelings. Similarly, we all experience the hero role when we are being rational and courageous in the face of pain and danger. Even the bully is regularly experienced in situations which encourage rational identification with the legal or social domination of a person, and one transgresses the defined or "acceptable" boundaries of that domination. The ordinary or typical identity states that one experiences in regard to these roles are fluctuating and temporary. But when one role is sustained and enacted unconsciously over and over again, it is surely part of a complex—a collection of images, feelings and habitual actions which are motivating in an unintended or impersonal way.

The intrapsychic experience of the hag is similar to the interpersonal one. The bully or hero side of the complex is then personified or imagined in animus or anima form. Usually, women experience the hag as a part of their self-hatred; the hag is motivated by an insistent animus complex that just "doesn't understand" and does not believe that the woman "makes sense" or is worthy of love. The animus can take the form of alien outsider, as bully or rapist. Or the animus can take the form of rational father, god or king (in modern life, the "authority" of the professor or executive). In men, the hag is the anima form of emotional accusation and impulsive outburst that comes to life in the face of some prematurely "rational" solution or naively "courageous" act. Similarly, the hag can be constellated as a man's anima state when he feels the threat of a real or imagined bully in himself or in the environment. It is my clinical experience that the hag, as an identity state, typically comes into being in middle life. For women, this identity state is connected to fears and shame regarding physical appearance (the idea of growing fat and old) or to fatigue in the care-giving role (the unappreciated mother). In men, the hag is often constellated in the condition of the "dying hero," due to fears concerning the overwhelming power of feeling life and unacknowledged dependencies.

I have wondered to what extent the anima-hag may contribute to diatribes against the women's movement, especially among middle-aged people who seem to advocate for women the Great Mother role as the sole life identity. Individuals' fears of suffocating, stagnating and depriving mothers are often summoned up, along with some supportive "data" or "studies" which "demonstrate" that women should necessarily be the primary providers of bonding relationships for the young of the species. While such arguments may seem rational on the surface, one does not have to scratch very deeply to see a non-rational element at work: the fear of the hag.

An example of this is in Anthony Stevens's otherwise commendable work, *Archetypes: A Natural History of the Self.* He has a chapter on the archetypal masculine and feminine in which he develops a position which is so naively irrational as to be an embarrassing piece of scholarship and politics.[5] I believe he is fearfully confronting the hag when he says such things as the following about women, in defense of their being biologically better suited to maternal roles than men:

> Women display a marked lack of enthusiasm for public affairs: for many years now it has been possible for them to enter politics as well as professional and business organizations, but seldom do they reach the pinnacles of power.[6]

And:

> Male dominance is by no means confined to politics. In all cultures, the creative artists, composers, scientists and philosophers are predominantly men, and overwhelmingly so. It is only in literature—presumably because of their superior verbal skills—and in the performing arts that women have made a significant contribution, though, here again, men are overwhelmingly in the ascendant. The women's movement would seek to explain this as the result of masculine "privilege" and the constraints imposed on women by male chauvinism. But this facile argument does not bear scrutiny. Even in those occupations which are

traditionally the métier of women—hairdressing, cookery, dress-making, and so on—it is men who are the innovators and chief exponents. In the arts, moreover, women have been encouraged to paint pictures and make music by their menfolk since the time of the Renaissance, yet, to date, there has been no woman Beethoven or Stravinsky, Picasso or Leonardo da Vinci.[7]

And finally:

> There are and always have been women of outstanding ability, but even the brightest of them seem to lack those para-intellectual qualities which determine success in creative work, namely, perseverance, aggression and ambition—all of which are known to be enhanced by the presence of testosterone in the bloodstream and are probably due to differences in cerebral development as well.[8]

These passages hardly merit serious commentary. If they had addressed the absence of black men among the Beethovens and philosophers of Western culture, they would have been so obviously racist as to be considered ridiculous in any serious analysis of intellectual history. I believe that Stevens is confronting the hag in the women's movement (who says "*I* know the answer") and is responding to her with the data he has gathered, much like the naive Arthur, seeking to maintain dominance of the decision-making domain. If this is not sufficient evidence of the non-rational masquerading as fact, consider a brief but intriguing slip in Stevens's attack on the women's movement. He uses the anthropological research of Beatrice Whiting to support his position that females across six cultures specialize in nurturance (from childhood onward) whereas males specialize in dominance. The element which reveals Stevens's blindness here is the fact that he assumes "B. Whiting" to be a man, noting, "He explained the traits as being indispensable to the development of skills appropriate to motherhood."[9] It is the self-protective orientation of *us versus them* which is at the core of modern problems with the negative mother complex.

When the complex dominates the interpersonal field of a couple relationship, basic trust is threatened. The couple risks losing the relationship, especially if the complex is the primary means by which they interact in the bedroom and in parenting. When trust in attachment relationships is threatened too often, it may disappear altogether. Feelings of self-hatred, self-protectiveness, aloneness and vengeance then replace basic trust, and the relationship turns into an arena of dominance-submission.

Conflict in itself is certainly not necessarily unhealthy in relationships. In fact, conflict can be both stimulating and informing for a couple. From our clinical experience, we see that conflict can take forms which are enhancing or threatening to basic trust. When conflict is enhancing, both partners in the couple—and the couple may be parent and child as well as partners—are able to listen and to empathize with each other, at least to some degree. When conflict is threatening, it is wholly ruled by unconscious complexes which are grander, meaner and more powerful than ordinary people can be.

5

Embracing the Hag in Middle Life

*An important requirement for treatment is the patient's
perception that it is he or she who must be changed in
some fundamental way. This motivation to work on the
inner issues which are seen as leading to the sense of
stagnation does not mean that character change, per se,
is the patient's goal. The patient sees that new life
choices are being blocked from within. Often there is
expressed concern with long-standing patterns of
behavior which are now seen as obstacles to growth.*
— "The Mid-Life Patient"[1]

Our story of Dame Ragnell's influence on Arthur and Gawain is
especially suitable for considering couples in middle life. Middle life
can be a chronological period or a state of mind. Typically the two
coincide in a particular kind of malaise that settles in some time
between the ages of thirty-five and fifty. In a couple relationship, the
malaise may emerge even earlier, depending on how long the couple
has been together and under what conditions. Feelings of despair,
resignation, bitterness and boredom characterize the day-to-day life
of such a couple. These feelings, imaged in the hag and bully roles
of the negative mother complex, are signs or symptoms that developmental issues of middle life are at hand. Especially the experience of
psychological stagnation can be recognized in the repeated entrap-
ments in the complex. The partners' idealizations of themselves and
each other were tarnished long ago, and their routine accusations of
hurt and anger have become veritable litanies that can be readily
recited by either member.

Assessing the Potential Loss

Both people know, consciously or unconsciously, that they are facing
profound loss. Recognizing and verbally acknowledging that loss is
the central motivating factor in the beginning of therapy with such a
couple. The potential loss of the cherished ties and shared values of
the relationship presents a shock to ordinary consciousness. The
shock of loss provokes a crisis which can lead to further individuation. Embedded in the threat of loss are fantasies (often childhood
fantasies) of one's own specialness, perfection, immortality and of

85

one's claim to complete security and understanding. These wishes for perfection and complete security typically obscure dark fears of one's hidden angry, shameful and destructive aspects. Embracing these hidden aspects of oneself becomes the vehicle for further development.

Jung maintained that the task of individuation in the second half of life is one of counterbalancing the one-sided achievements of the first half. Individuation, understood here as the successive integration of unconscious complexes into conscious identity, and hence the engendering of a dialectic between personal and archetypal realities, has a common set of characteristics in middle life. These characteristics take on different forms with different people, but tend to concern two areas of personality functioning: loss-separation and self-esteem. In midlife, under the felt pressure that time is "running out," people are vulnerable to depression about lost possibilities. Both oneself and others, especially intimate others, are perceived as "less than" one hoped they would be. Fears of loss, abandonment and separation—especially prominent in women—exacerbate the feelings of helplessness or hopelessness about the future.

The typical psychodynamic issues of midlife were addressed in a classic article by psychiatrist Elliot Jaques.[2] He described the process of coming to terms with the limitations in one's own goodness and power, as well as in the goodness and power of others. One's own hateful, destructive and enraged feelings have been partly concealed by "impossible wishes" from childhood, the wishes for perfection, total responsiveness from others, choices free of conflict and pain, and complete fulfillment. The major developmental task, according to Jaques, is to accept the realistic imperfections of human life in the context of "faith" or meaning. Hope for humanity and support of future generations contribute to transcendence of the bitterness and rage stemming from the infantile childhood wishes. The hoped-for outcome of the midlife crisis is "resignation without despair."

Jung articulated the process of individuation in middle life as mainly concerned with the integration of the contrasexual side of one's own personality. Specifically, he contended that men had to integrate their "repressed feminine" aspects, called the anima, while women would have to integrate the "repressed masculine," or animus. These contrasexual elements were discussed in chapter two as complexes of ideas, images, feelings and action which have been organized around the excluded aspects of one's gender identity. Typically for men, the integration of the anima entails movement away from identification with being an independent, autonomous hero and movement toward dependence (as *inter*dependence) and an expressive feeling life. For women, the situation is somewhat the reverse: integration of the animus usually requires a shift from a more dependent and accommodative identity as nurturer and mediator of others' development toward a more authoritative, agentive embrace of one's own development. To put this another way, Jung asserted that development in middle and later life depended on changing one's earlier adaptation and consciously including much of what had been previously relegated to habit and dependency, through projection and expectations from others.

As mentioned earlier, Gutmann has contributed empirical evidence of this kind of shift in adaptation.[3] From cross-cultural studies of men and women in the second half of life, he discovered that men tended to move from active to more accommodative-passive modes of behaving, while women moved in the opposite direction. From Jung's perspective, and essential to our understanding of couple relationships, this movement must take place consciously and not merely as an unconscious adaptive pattern. Individuals must integrate into their personal awareness the ideals and values, as well as some of the actions and skills, that are connected to the "other side" of their gender identity (and previously projected onto the other sex).

When a couple is caught in the negative mother complex, the motivation to work on the inner issues which block trust in one's partner appears to emerge directly from the confrontation with the potential loss of the relationship. It is the voice of the hag which will express the "truth" of their situation: she will say, however hesitantly or conflictually, that her husband has much to lose if he does not embrace a more personal feeling life. She may say this nonverbally by withdrawing from him sexually, or she may say it impulsively by seeking another lover or by covertly encouraging her children to challenge her partner's authority. She recognizes that she "has the answer" to the dilemma of their situation, but she will have little confidence that her ideas are worthwhile or even sensible. Giving the hag a voice is the first step in working with a couple who is trapped in the negative mother complex. We must simultaneously give the hero an ear or a mode for understanding the feminine perspective that the hag is trying to articulate.

Recognition of potential loss, for the man, is usually best formulated as a loss of property and paternity rights. He will lose his wife and children, his position in the family and his house or other financial assets. He may also lose a good cook, a skilled household manager, a good friend and the social network which typically has been sustained by his wife's efforts over the years. More abstractly, but still rationally, he will lose the opportunity to be an intimate and valued member of his family and to guide his children securely into the future. Initially, the man will usually denigrate any explanation of the threat of personal loss to his own inner life, to his creative expression and to his yet unlived potential.

Recognition of potential loss for the woman is generally best articulated as a loss of valued relationships. She will lose the relationship she has established with her husband and some of the friends they have in common. Depending on the degree of the woman's depression and the profundity of her identification with the hag, she may or may not be able to acknowledge the potential loss of her own female adulthood. Often the resentment and bitterness of the hag identification have become an ironclad defense against any claim to self-worth, enthusiasm about her skills and competence, or ability to envision a revitalization of her own femaleness.

The story of Sir Gawain and the Lady Ragnell provides us with three successive frames for envisioning the development of the couple from basic mistrust to the re-establishment of trust. The three frames reflect the gradual retreat of dominance-submission themes of power and the gradual appearance of attachment-separation themes of love. They can be used therapeutically as a guide in helping couples change and gain insight into development in middle life. The first frame is characterized by the desire for possession and dominance, the second by understanding the repressed feminine, and the third by the power of free choice in love.

Dominance and Possession

The original spell cast by Gromer on Ragnell can be interpreted as the spell cast by marriage itself through the desire to dominate or be dominated. How do power problems intersect with health and happiness in marriage? From our story, we can answer that the precondition to vitality in intimate relationship between adults is sovereignty over one's own life. Sovereignty in intimate relationship is founded on a recognition of interdependence, on reciprocity based on mutual trust, and not on the dominance of one individual over another.

In actuality, the institution of marriage has never been effectively binding on a man's freedom, his monogamy, his responsibility for financial support of wife or children, or on his commitment to romantic love with his wife. Consequently, the problem of dominance-submission tends to focus on the man's dominance and the woman's submission in traditional marriage. In her recent study of married and single people, Jessie Bernard showed that single women are healthier and happier than their married counterparts on a variety of indices which measure symptoms of psychological distress, mental health impairment, physical health, income, crime, suicide and alcoholism.[4] On the same indices, husbands were found to be generally both healthier and happier than their wives. Legal and financial power belongs preponderately to the husband in traditional marriage. Even this legal or financial sovereignty seems to result in greater health and happiness for the husband than for the wife.

Within the legal institution of marriage, the woman intentionally or unconsciously submits to an inferior position in regard to the development of authority and competence in her own life. This submission eventually leads to unhappiness, especially during middle life, when the woman must actualize what has been repressed in her own identity. Furthermore, if the woman can experience no value or legitimate authority in her own accomplishments, usually in the area of care-giving and relational skills, then her self-esteem will become quite low. Low self-esteem and inferior social status combine to confront the woman with a loss of vitality and lack of belief in the promise of the future. Reasonable fears about career incompetence, identification with inferior human qualities, and unpredictable anxiety due to the negative mother complex in family life tend to produce a feeling of helplessness in the woman. This feeling increasingly dominates the interpersonal field of the couple relationship. Simultaneously, the middle-aged man may face disappointments deriving from his early dreams for achievement and for perfectly satisfying relationships. Depression in both partners is often the most obvious presenting problem in the midlife couple seeking psychotherapy.

As long as the man continues to dominate the decision-making and authority-engendering positions in the couple relationship, the partners will continue to enact the negative mother complex and experience increasing despair about escaping from it. Although the man may consider domination to be part of his social role and prerogative as husband, he must be shown that the vitality of adult bonding is threatened by dominance-submission routines. Only the threat of personal loss is likely to propel a dominant husband into a conscious recognition of the value of equality for relational interdependence.

Let us trace some of the assumptions of the ideal of equality in adult bonding in order to clarify the background of the interpersonal issues facing a couple when domination is the central interpersonal struggle. Attachment and trust are engendered through mutuality and reciprocity based on secure individual identity. In order to trust another person as a strong and independent other, one must first be free oneself. A precondition of mutual adult bonding thus seems to be individuality of one's own. Sullivan discovered that relationship between equals typically forms for the first time among peers in

Polly never talks about How to get there first.

pre-adolescence and adolescence. He talks about the "chum" relationship as the necessary foundation for mature love. Whereas we
develop nurturant-attachment behaviors and dominance-submission
behaviors in parent-child relationships, we develop reciprocal trust
only in relationships of equality. Reciprocal trust is grounded in the
experience of being able to consider another's needs and attitudes to
be as legitimate and worthwhile as one's own (not more or less so).

Sullivan's discovery regarding mature love has been elaborated,
in a somewhat different form, by Jean Piaget through his studies of
the development of justice and morality in children.[5] Piaget discovered that the ideals of equality and justice come directly from peer
relationships, not from the relationships of subordinates to authority
figures (such as parents and teachers). Peer play forces children to
recognize the meaning of trust, honesty and fairness, and not simply
to give obedient lip service to these principles in imitation of their
parents.

In working with couples, we have discovered anew the importance of teaching people, through their own experience in therapy,
that *sharing* tasks of daily living and family life relates directly to
each partner's respect for the other as an equal. Equality between
adults means consistent validation of each other's personal authority,
worth and competence on a day-to-day basis. Equality does not
require, however, that each individual participate equally in all of
the tasks involved. Individuals may specialize in providing certain
tasks (e.g., in managing children, nurturing or breadwinning), but
each person respects the other's strengths and trusts the other to
make choices regarding his or her own destiny as an individual.

When a couple enters therapy under the shadow of dominance,
the wife has recognized the sham of her dependence. She already
knows, although she may not verbalize it directly, that she cannot
thrive in an atmosphere of implied inferiority or dependence. She is
consciously allied with the hag. The hag has a bitter, complaining,
independent voice—"Only *I* know the answer." The husband cannot
rationally analyze what is "wrong" with his assumption that he
"should" provide the decision making, secure the financial arrangements or expect to be treated as the superior member due to his
courageous heroic stance in the world—to his willingness to "go out
there and fight" for the survival of his family. Furthermore, he
cannot experience the problem of his wife's despair as having anything to do with him. Although he may have temper tantrums (often
called "bottled-up rage"), manage the children aggressively and fail
to be of value to his wife, he does not see any association between
these experiences and his role as the dominant partner in the relationship. The therapists will often discover that this man is emotion-

ally isolated, guilty and even sad, although he claims not to have such feelings. From his heroic perspective, he will deny these feelings and only claim the abstract principles of his "right" to be treated with respect and love as the breadwinner and leader of his pack. Although his own anima complex may behave in quite irrational ways, he will project this onto his wife, who is quite willing to be understood as "crazy."

The vital emotional field between the members of this couple, at the stage of dominance-submission, is loss. Loss is the experience of separating from something or someone that has been valued and included as a part of oneself, as a part of one's own personality. Usually the wife experiences this somewhat consciously while the husband experiences it unconsciously. The therapists will recognize the loss of self-esteem in the wife as an initial feature in her self-presentation. They can anticipate that the man will experience a drop in his self-esteem initially when he confronts the repressed feminine in himself. The situation cannot be otherwise because he will face the angry, shameful and destructive elements in himself, as well as the prospect of taking on roles and attitudes which are not rewarded openly by our society.

The challenge to the man in this phase of therapy is to face those hidden, destructive parts of himself that he has projected onto his wife and children. The challenge to the woman is to be more agentive in her unclaimed authority and competence—to face the repressed feminine in herself.

Understanding the Repressed Feminine

A shift to the second stage of therapy, to the frame in which Ragnell challenges the authority of the king openly and Gawain willingly takes on the task of embracing the hag, is especially difficult for the man. On the surface, it looks as though all privilege and power are on his side. What increase in self-esteem or social status could a man gain by developing a feeling life or acknowledging his dependence on wife and children? Men who are consciously identified with the bully or hero role may even ask, "What will I gain by changing?" The therapists must respond with another question: "What will you lose by not changing?"

The emphasis must remain on loss, in regard to the man, and the therapists must illustrate in detail the shocking losses which are in store for the man if he does not face what has been repressed in himself. As the Colemans say in their study of "dyadic" or shared parenting, the man faces the greater challenge at this point:

He must give up some of the prerogatives that society has placed in highest esteem. The dyadic father must accept a limitation on his career, for he can no longer expect unequivocal support and self-sacrifice from his mate when needs on the job interfere with life at home.... If a man expects marriage to be an intense, ongoing relationship that penetrates all areas of his experience, the constraints will feel like the "work" that achieves this goal.[6]

The man will need empathic support in facing his situation squarely. His wife should be his major supporter in making the changes in their relationship. The therapists will help her claim her own authority and competence in doing so.

When the woman has found an authoritative voice (the voice of Ragnell when she challenges the king), several conditions operate which are different from the earlier phase of dominance-submission. The woman is now a more confident hag and the man is a rational, courageous hero. Whereas the woman has substantially overcome her feelings of hopelessness about herself, she does not yet feel womanly or trust her partner's love. In the story, the situation is depicted as follows: Ragnell's answer has saved the king's head and she has won Gawain; now they are at the wedding banquet surrounded by courtiers who do not understand the situation of their relationship. Ragnell is certain she has a secret that will lead to imtimacy between herself and Gawain, but she is not able to reach the vitality of her own hidden "princess" identity. This is the configuration of many "liberated" couples who enter therapy.

The liberated wife has returned to college, or she has gone back to her career or otherwise learned to believe in her own values and legitimacy as an individual. She has assigned chores to her partner and organized her household around her new goals. She has a sense of agency, but still she feels bitter and unloved as well as depreciated or undervalued by "the neighbors." The chances of failure in the development of such a couple are still very high because, although they appear to be on the road to equality and vitality, they experience themselves as unable to join in a clear partnership.

From the story we know this: the hag must refuse lip service to her demands and must not give in to the collective signals that she is inferior or domineering. She must continue to act confidently on her intuition that her partner has not fully embraced her or the household. This is difficult both for the woman and for the therapists who are assisting her because the rational arguments of the heroic Gawain often sound very convincing.

The Gawain hero appears to be open to his partner's ideas and initiative because he continually asks, "What does she really want?" Although he appears to be reasonable and concerned, the therapists will discover that he does not really listen to what he is told, either by his partner or by the therapists. He argues rationally that he cannot see much sense in opening himself to the non-rational world of communication or experience (e.g., to understanding his dreams), and he may retreat into the bully posture of Gromer if he is pushed too far without adequate support.

In one couple seen by my partner and me, this kind of retreat to the bully posture was evident in the fourth session of therapy, just as we had begun to believe that the couple had changed substantially. In the third session, the wife had spoken of her desire for more emotional openness between them and asked for an agreement that she and her husband talk more openly about their ideas on parenting their stepson (his son by a previous marriage). She requested that her husband support her in having the son help more in tasks around the house. In prior sessions, the husband had been reluctant to give up his intimacy with his son, enacted as an unconscious father-son alliance against the wife. In addition, the husband had repeatedly argued rationally that talking about feelings did not help. He believed the therapists were "churning up dissension" by supporting his wife's desire for more discussion of their emotional life. But the husband agreed, in the third session, to some specific arrangements concerning how he and his wife would be partners in parenting the boy.

When he got home, however, he immediately told his son that only he was "giving orders around here" and virtually cut off any relationship of trust and respect between the son and his stepmother. During the fourth session, the wife could hardly speak; in place of her words there were tears and heavy sighs. She was back out in the woods and her husband now stated very rationally that the therapists' plan "had not worked," and that he was "sure that his wife would never be able to be comforted" in regard to the son because she was "jealous" of the relationship he had established over the years with the boy. He had used his bullying defeat of the therapy plan as "proof" that we were all wrong and that his wife was a virtual outsider to their family. The husband seemed bitterly triumphant about his demonstration of our failure and was openly contemptuous of our alleged expertise.

Our strategy in such a retreat to the bully posture is to beat the hero at his own game. Because the heroic stance is backed by the world of facts and the ideals of rational proof, we offer results from many studies which support the viability of equal partnership in carrying out the ordinary tasks of care-giving. Studies which show that men are as capable as women in care-giving and relationship can be the backbone of therapy with the hero at this stage. While the hero wishes to understand what the woman wants, behind the heroic stance is the defensive conviction that neither her words nor her world "make sense." "Biology is destiny" is the implicit argument backing many men's seemingly rational position. They believe that women are just naturally better suited to emotional expression and care-giving. Indeed, this belief also includes the assumption that the feminine skills of care-giving simply emerge full-blown in women and are not the result of special training or learned expertise. The belief that women are natural care-givers, that care-giving involves no special learning or development, and that it is inferior to other kinds of achievement of rational expression and decision making is problematic for both members of a couple. "Biology is destiny" means essentially that *female* biology is destiny and that its expression is undifferentiated. Such beliefs are the product of the repressed feminine in individual women and men, as well as the result of the oppression of women in our society.

Although hormones and brain structures are clearly different in men and women, the differences do not prevent men from responding tenderly, from learning the skills of care-giving, from weeping or from valuing their dependence on others. All of us are capable of mothering and attachment behaviors although we may have different thresholds for the stimulation and release of nurturant, tender responses. John Money, a psychologist who has extensively studied the development of gender identity in human males and females, believes that most sex-different behaviors (with the exception of the male ability to impregnate and menstruation, gestation and lactation in the female) are potentially sex-shared. He says:

> Almost all behavioral sex differences will be understood not as absolutes, but as relative to the strength of the threshold that regulates their manifestation. In other words, most apparently sex-different behavior will actually be sex-shared, but threshold different.[7]

Money has studied many variations of the typical hormonal sex-differentiation patterns and has concluded that socialization plays a stronger part in gender identity than biology does. The two interact inextricably, of course, in any individual's life, but Money has discovered that peoples' attributions and constructs about "male" and "female" behaviors and attitudes are a much stronger force in shaping identity than are hormones and genital structures. He gives the following case of nurturant behavior in laboratory male rats:

> You can get nest building and retrieving of the young even from a recalcitrant male rat that never likes to look after young ones, if every day for a week, more or less, you assiduously put a new litter in with

him.... Finally, he starts to build a nest, hover over the young, re-trieve them, and look after them. It's the same kind of parental behavior that the female shows.[8]

Surely, if there is an archetype of the Great Mother among male rats, there must be one among human males. Such a study demon-strates that attachment and nurturant behaviors are not biologically confined to females; they are socially confined.

Studies by the Harlows are equally instructive for the heroic husband who needs convincing.[9] They found that although mon-key mothers spontaneously care for their infants immediately after their birth, their care-taking is apparently the product of social influences rather than biological imperatives. In the laboratory, they produced female monkeys who were woefully inadequate moth-ers by removing them from their own mothers at birth and rearing them in isolation. When these isolated females were impregnated, they failed to perform normal maternal functions and even turned aggressively on their young. Among monkeys, as well as among humans, learning to love is an experience that comes from early bonding as well as from continuing interactions in relationships throughout life.

Through her study of the Manus of New Guinea, Margaret Mead discovered a culture in which men played an important part in the nurturing of babies.[10] The men in this culture played with the chil-dren and seemed content to do so (after early morning fishing) while the women worked. The mothers trained the children to avoid cer-tain dangers, by teaching babies to cling to the neck of an adult and not to fall in the water or touch the fire. Not surprisingly, Mead found that the children were attentive and joyous around their fa-thers and generally avoided their mothers. Mothers were often abused in front of the children by the men and the men's relatives, and the children developed a strong allegiance to the father. When Mead brought dolls into this setting, the boys spontaneously played with them more than the girls did.

This kind of evidence shows only the potential for care-giving and nurturing behaviors that can be developed in males as well as fe-males. In our society, as in most developed societies, adult males rarely participate intimately in these activities. Because the care-giving activities are not reinforced by money or status, even when they are professionally provided (e.g., in professions like teaching, nursing and social work), little attention is paid to the competence and skills involved in the activities and much is assumed about the inherited capacity to carry them out.

Revaluing the tasks of ordinary care-giving is a process, first, of claiming the worth and complexity of these activities, and then of deciding how they will be shared. More often than not, the liberated or feminist couples who have sought therapy with us have failed to complete the first step. Consequently, neither person feels much personal worth or significance in carrying out the ordinary tasks of care-giving. Embracing the repressed feminine entails understanding the oppression of women, the value of care-giving activities and the complexity and competence associated with them, as well as integrating the feminine elements of one's own personality. For both men and women, this can be an ambivalent process.

In the Gawain-hag configuration of the negative mother complex, the woman remains primarily in the hag identity while her husband appears to be adapting to her demands. Actually, he is only paying lip service to an ideal, and both people repeatedly experience the deception in his pretense even though they may not be able to articulate it. The woman presents herself as primarily indifferent to the earlier attractions of her role as wife and lover, as mother and nurturer. She may be indifferent to sex, and she is surely indifferent to the promises of jewels, land or other wealth that the man has offered in exchange for her servitude. Although she may unconsciously feel the conviction of her position ("I have the answer"), she will doubt it consciously. Doubt of the reality of her own experience, and of her desire to value her care-giving skills and emotional life, can lead to a belief that she is "going crazy." Because she also knows "the facts" of the social world around her and acknowledges the importance of rationality, she will find the non-rationality of her own position very troubling. How can she continue to be such a nag when her husband appears to be doing everything that she asks of him? She feels guilty about her own experience and ashamed of the rage and anger that seem to pull at her through most of the day. Actually, she may desire more autonomy and freedom in her sense of self (the integration of the animus), but she is unable to trust these desires, just as she is unable to trust her partner's "good faith" in embracing her and her world.

Usually, this lack of trust extends further and becomes a generalized perspective on men, and even on other women. In her hag identity, the woman believes that no one has the ability to understand her overwhelming feelings of inherent unworthiness, stupidity and ugliness. She may even appear to others to cherish her unhappy lot and to have an ideal of self-hatred, pain and suffering.

Just as the man needs rational arguments to awaken his understanding of the feminine within himself and others, so the woman needs a rational voice that convincingly expresses the worth and complexity of the non-rational world. At this point, when she is still hag-identified but feeling more forceful and independent, the therapists can give her words. This does not mean that she is told what to think, but rather that rational arguments and empirical evidence are offered to show her that she indeed has a powerful position as care-giver. She will be especially impressed to hear her unspoken ideas traced out in an heroic framework which seems convincing to her husband. Both the validity of her suffering and the complexity of her role need to be articulated in the context of the larger social themes of the oppression of women and the lack of opportunity for men to become care-givers.

What we typically discover when we present the data for the legitimacy of the non-rational world is that both people are relieved. The man is relieved to discover that his wife is not crazy and that she has good reason to feel hurt, angry and isolated. The woman is relieved to discover that she has intuitively been accurate in refusing to believe that her husband's embrace of her world was complete. It is at this point that we can collaborate to arrive at solutions to the problems of sharing care-giving tasks.

Equality, mutuality and sharing in a couple relationship cannot be accomplished at a rational level. A major roadblock to trust develops around the scheduling of household chores and child care in terms of "you take out the garbage on Mondays and Wednesdays and I will do the laundry on Thursdays and Saturdays." This kind of schedule may be a final outcome of a process of collaboration, but the process must be the continual living arena, not the schedule. Reciprocity based on trust is not rational problem-solving or deci-sion-making activity. Rather, it is the ongoing understanding and acceptance of another's strengths, talents, needs and capacities, in the context of one's own strengths, talents, needs and capacities. At any given moment, this kind of reciprocity rarely results in 50-50 sharing. Sometimes one partner appears to give more and be more inconvenienced; at other times, it is the reverse. Illness, personal exigencies, real abilities and personal interests have always to be understood in the moment. Similarly, insight, good luck, inspiration and pleasure have a part in each person's ability to give and to receive help. It is a fact that no formula for working out equality will help; only a commitment to trusting the other person and oneself as partners can be a viable basis for embracing the repressed feminine.

Commitment to understanding another person and to cherishing the other person's individuality as much as one's own is a continuing life process; rational planning and scheduling are only a part of the struggle. The ongoing archetypal problem of adult attachment—reci-procity based on trust—requires the kind of self-scrutiny and accept-ance that are the groundwork for individuation. Any verbal discussion of this struggle is ultimately inadequate to its description because of the very nature of language; words make discrete references and their structure is largely rational and sequential. Thus, it is difficult to teach a couple about this issue of reciprocity; they must experience it through their own struggle to revalue the hidden, shameful, angry, emotional and weak elements in themselves.

To some extent, the practical realities of life seem at odds with the embrace of the feminine in the current social context of our lives. Because this revaluing takes time and energy that would otherwise be spent outside of home and family or simply in "mindless chores," couples must initially schedule time to work through their differences. This scheduling of intimate time also seems incongruent with the task of re-establishing trust and commitment. We have not discovered any way to get around this initially because couples who are enacting the negative mother complex have turned their lives into battle lines and separate existences. Eventually, the time set aside for working-through becomes more organic and seems to have a life of its own. It demands their attention because they want to maintain an atmosphere of trust between them.

Usually the man will initially support the idea of scheduling regular intimate times with his partner in order to come to terms with this problem of broken trust, but he will then find these times are empty for him. Usually he has more resistance toward revaluing the feminine aspects of his life because he has resisted feeling the pain, especially the hurt, in himself and others. The heroic Gawain-husband presents himself as an empty hero; he is willing but stupid. This is the crux (or the curse) of the matter for him. He may see himself as a "liberated" male, but he does not turn his intelligence to the feminine, neither to the ordinary matters of daily living, nor to the non-rational meaning of what his wife presents to him. He really has refused to listen. When he feels himself pushed too far emotionally, he can retreat into the bully posture.

In speaking about the struggle toward more dyadic or shared parenting, the Colemans say the following:

> To work on deep, intrapsychic levels, dyadic parenting needs myths, images and legends, gods and goddesses, sacred couples, androgynous images—it needs support on an unconscious level as well as on a conscious level.
>
> When two people must work together as one, it is not easy to synchronize decisions, balance schedules, agree on tactics, and share benefits. In parenting this may seem especially complicated, because it touches emotions and attitudes that were established in childhood and may not be within reach of conscious thought. These unconscious assumptions may affect the way a man and a woman relate to each

other as parents very differently than they affect the way they relate
to each other as lovers or as husband and wife. Girls are more likely
to have been socialized to expect parenting to be a marital and a life
task than boys; therefore, the experience of the dyadic parent is likely
to be more radical for the men.[11]

What the Colemans refer to here as "parenting" is, for us, the
feminine: the ability to respond openly and accurately to another's
needs and to the nurturant environment in its totality. We have
discovered that this ability intersects remarkably with satisfaction in
all areas of intimate relating in a middle life couple. Sexual intimacy, emotional security and trust, and interpersonal respect are all
affected by each person's willingness to value and turn intelligence
toward the nurturant capacity in self and others.

We have come to see Gawain's final embrace of Ragnell as the
true heroic act. The courage to open oneself to the dreaded and
feared hag, to the potential flood of destruction and disintegration
she represents (sucking out the soul), is genuinely heroic. When a
man opens himself to this kind of relationship to himself and others,
he inevitably experiences depression. Because of his social position
and his habitual denial of dependence and weakness, the situation
cannot be otherwise. Negative social pressures and the experience of
guilt are involved in embracing the hag. Yet to refuse her embrace
will mean an even more profound loss, the loss of his own further
development and probably the loss of any intimate vitality with his
wife in later life.

Some healthy defenses against the onslaught of depression can be
established. Support from other men, for example in an organized
men's support group, is helpful in combating the doubts and fears
the man will experience. The therapeutic use of empirical studies
and rational argument will broaden the social context of male gender identity for the man. Initially, we use these rational tools to
defeat or outwit the man's defenses and make him more vulnerable
to the hag in his wife. Near the end of the second phase of therapy,
when the man needs to internalize the values of women and the
feminine in himself, we use the arguments again to bolster his position
and to support his further development. Developing an openness to
the feminine in oneself and the world is non-adaptive for men; if they
are identified with traditional cultural values, they will feel at odds
with the collective ideals of masculine superiority. Kissing the hag is a
difficult heroic act and one that must be enacted repeatedly in a society that attributes superiority to males and inferiority to females.

What do women really want? Through the story, we discover that
it is the right to sovereignty over their own lives. This is no simple

matter since it demands partnership with men. True sovereignty rests on trust of both oneself and the other. This trust entails commitment to reciprocity. In order to enact this ideal, one must be an individual, responsible for one's own development, and a social being who appreciates the interdependence of human life. Individualism is not the final goal of women's desire for sovereignty. If the story had depicted a simple liberation of Ragnell from Gromer's spell, we would not have found it a fitting mystery for the development of a couple relationship. In the end, Ragnell is dependent on Gawain's acknowledgment of her independence and on his commitment to it. In turn, Gawain is dependent on Ragnell's trust that he can come to this acknowledgment on his own; she would not have chosen him if it were otherwise.

The man's fear that a woman wants to dominate his life is a childish fear of the powerful mother complex, projected almost entirely onto a woman. In fact, women seem to depend a great deal on their reflection from another for a healthy sense of self-worth. Obviously, they can become too dependent on this approval and thus carry a childish wish to be secure in it, without the conflicts which attend responsibility for independence. Ultimately, it seems that the desire for sovereignty expressed by Ragnell is a desire that men truly listen and understand the experience of women and the oppression of the feminine in our world.

Love and Free Choice

The final phase of the Gawain-Ragnell encounter occurs after Gawain's initial embrace of the hag. He sees the potential for the vital feminine in his wife (the princess), but he is faced with a choice. The choice is a test, unknown to him, of the depth of his commitment to Ragnell's independence. The wonders of beauty, as power, are the focus of the story: Gawain must decide whether his woman would be beautiful in the castle by day and display to his friends her lovely charms, or whether she would be beautiful in their chamber at night so that he could embrace her in her real form.

These two polarities of feminine beauty, the public power and the private pleasure, are often defensively split in men's experience of real women. The man who seeks the moral, gracious and educated strong woman "by day" (in his normal consciousness) may discover that he cannot be intimate with her "by night" (in his instinctual depths). The darker, mysterious and uneducated woman—called an "island woman" by one of my analysands—may become the focus of his sexual feelings.

The split between the powers of women by day and their powers by night has been and continues to be a problem for men in devel-

oping intimate relationships with women, especially when they are
in the throes of a mother complex. In our story, Gawain encounters
this problem in a koan-like challenge and is able to solve it simply.
In real couples, this challenge is an ongoing problem with men who
must contend with their feminism in public and private life. Traditionally, the wife is the man's property, and her beauty, charm and
graciousness express *his* good taste and accomplishments. If a man's
wife seems too independent, his dignity is threatened and he must
retreat publicly. If a man grants his wife independence and then
finds that she becomes a powerful person in her own right, he may
feel his sexual dominion threatened, and hence become impotent in
her presence. What the story suggests, and what we experience in
working with couples in middle life, is that the restoration of a
woman's vitality and beauty occurs through her partner's validation
of her own authority over her life.

Even in a single therapy session, we have seen visible signs of the
transformation of a confused, tearful and resentful hag to a confident, vital princess of steadfast insight. This kind of instantaneous
change is not immediately integrated, however, and can quickly
fade. Still, the change in a woman's appearance, voice and manner
can be noted and emphasized quite early in the process of restoring
trust. Neither the hag nor the princess is an enduring identity state
in an adult woman. Both are unconscious complexes, organized
around archetypal images; they are transitory states in daily life. The
princess identity of being a beautiful, vital and cherished woman is
essential for a woman's self-esteem as she ages: the more she spontaneously feels this way, the more she will be able to believe in her
worth and goodness on an ongoing basis. This belief in her own
goodness is the crucial issue for her development in middle life. The
complete absence of the princess identity, in an older woman, is a
sign that she is depressed and that she has stagnated in her development.

What is symbolized in the final sequence in our story, in the
transformation of Ragnell into a clear-eyed young woman, is the
power of choice. Gawain is faced with a dilemma which is unsolva-
ble by rational means, that is, by weighing the benefits of alternatives. If he had made the choice *for* Ragnell (if he had stated *his*
preference), he would have lost. Instead of trying to work out an
individual solution, based on his own needs and wishes, Gawain
trusted Ragnell with the freedom and responsibility of her own
choice. Similarly, Ragnell would have remained forever entrapped in
the spell if Gawain had chosen for her; she had to have her own
right to choose freely restored to her before she could become her
true, vital self.

The process that began with Ragnell's claiming her own haggish authority ("*I* have the answer"), and with Gawain's efforts to understand, culminates in the man's recognition of his dependence on a woman (a person in her own right) and the woman's acknowledgment of her own responsibility for her life. This embrace of the repressed feminine is liberating for both partners. Although it might seem ideal if Ragnell could somehow come to her own legitimate sense of choice, without Gawain's blessing, our story states the situation otherwise. When the man begins by taking possession of the woman, through marriage, and the woman begins with the idea that she will be possessed, then the man must acknowledge his dependence on her, and she must acknowledge her trust of him in restoring her freedom. Perhaps we could abstractly trace the line of this development back to some mythical beginning of human culture when men overtook women with their physical strength, but this kind of analysis is unnecessary in the context of working with couples. Whether or not a woman could potentially restrain herself from projecting her personal authority onto a man (or men) is an abstraction. The fact is that most women do project this authority, and most men do assume that women *should.*

In the end, however, the union of the knightly Gawain and the princess Ragnell is a recognition that autonomy and empathy go hand in hand. Dependence and independence are not separate states, but are the polarities of human love. Embracing the hag in oneself or another means giving voice to one's hurt, anger and weakness. Allowing these voices to speak does not result in undifferentiated rage or tirade, but engenders sensitive and responsive empathy with their meaning. Coming to terms with the buried feminine or matriarchal culture means turning attention and intelligence to the dependence we all have on each other. Caring for people and things around us cannot be relegated to unconscious, habitual "mechanisms" constructed around fears and wishes. Nor can the caring be relegated to women alone. The road out of the woods, and the alienation of the hag and the bully, is to be found through the voice of the hag. Empathizing with her, by validating her experience and her suffering, results in the revitalization of relational life.

Let us return, now, to Louise and Larry in order to understand how this reconciliation might actually take place in a relationship.

Louise and Larry Embrace the Hag

Through a number of difficult sessions with Larry, focused especially on breaking through his rational defenses against the reality of Louise's emotional expressions, the therapists were able to show Larry how impossible his attitude had been. Although he repeatedly demanded that the therapists and Louise tell him what to do about his wife's unhappiness, he denigrated every idea we offered. He repeatedly denied the worth of feeling life ("That's just not the way I think. It means nothing to me and I can't just take your words or your experiences when they don't fit me."). Furthermore, he was a constant critic of Louise's mothering ("She's always trying to control the kids; I don't think she can stand to be with them more than fifteen minutes at a time. And for heaven's sake, it couldn't take much time to cook a real dinner occasionally. I'm so tired of eating those frozen dinners.").

Although he criticized Louise, he did not indicate through his daily actions that he was willing to rearrange his schedule so that he could learn more about cooking and cleaning in order to share it ("What am I supposed to do? I work all day. Should I cook dinner during my lunch break? If I quit working, we'd all starve anyway because she doesn't make enough money to support half a person, let alone a family of four."). Larry denigrated the skills associated with nurturance and refused to participate in the activities, but he constantly returned to a rational posture ("If I could only understand what to do to make her happy, I would do it, believe me.").

Through the help of the therapists, Larry finally realized that his fully grown-up wife would probably leave him if he didn't change. Whether she left the children or took them with her, clearly his life would change immensely on her departure. He began to acknowledge that he depended on her ("I really like a lot of things you do with the kids. I don't think they could have gotten through school without your help."). In a tearful session, Larry finally confronted his own refusal of the feminine aspects in himself and his projection of responsibility for his feeling and creative life onto Louise ("I am ashamed of how dependent and lazy I've been in regard to our friends, the church and even the kids. I don't really think I've been much of a father, but I thought you would take care of all the stuff with the kids. Sometimes I'm afraid I am a complete failure—at my work and at home. I haven't achieved what I wanted, and most of what I do at work seems empty. You and the kids are always squabbling and I know that I shouldn't just try to forget it, but that's what I do.").

Larry acknowledged his underlying wish for a perfectly responsive mother who would silently and willingly meet his every need. He also revealed previously hidden feelings of sadness, anger and shame regarding what he thought were failures in his career and in his role as a grown man in a family. Finally, when the therapists suggested it, Larry acknowledged that he had secretly thought his wife and children were inferior to himself in many ways. He had secretly believed they should be grateful that he provided for them in *whatever* way he offered, whether or not what he offered was responsive to their needs.

After acknowledging his dependency needs and his secret feelings of failure, Larry turned to Louise for support. Louise was quick to respond openly and positively to Larry's vulnerabilities. She offered to help him become more integrated into family life. Consequently, Larry took on some tasks around the house, at first under Louise's guidance, and developed considerable skill in cooking. As he began to revalue the ordinary tasks of living, he discovered new meaning in family life and found that his children were eager to idealize him and to seek his guidance.

Louise, initially through much assistance, eventually believed enough in her experience to retrieve some words (other than "I don't know") to meet Larry's rational challenges. She formulated a position regarding the importance of emotional expressiveness and asked for time to be with Larry alone so that they could share more of their inner lives. We asked Louise to guide some parts of our sessions and to show us what she wanted from Larry. She learned about her own competence and authority in interpreting non-rational communication. Both in and out of the sessions, she developed a greater appreciation for her "woman's intuition" and for the new kinds of insight she could bring to her relationship and her own life. During the sessions, we supported and elaborated her ideas in such a way that she came to claim her authority.

Eventually, this process of claiming her own knowledge and skills resulted in a confrontation with depression over the "lost possibilities" in her life. She spoke of her stupidity, her lack of education and her fears of competing with others whenever there was potential for conflict. In these encounters, we continued to emphasize her strengths and her achievements in relational life, and we sought to connect her with a better image of her own mother (whom she had seen as weak and dependent). Finally, Louise began to inquire into her own needs, especially her desires for sexual intimacy. She was disappointed in their sex life and wanted to be more sexually expressive with Larry. He was enthusiastic about this, but we kept to Louise's lead. She talked about her sexual excitement in their courtship days ("I used to get so turned on with all that petting"), and we suggested that they return to that level of interaction. The social constraints of their courtship—necking in secret places and caressing each other through clothing—had liberated her budding sexuality. Recovering some of the mystery of the courtship period finally evolved into Louise's confrontation with her own body ("I hate it").

Louise's work with her body and her sexuality was a crucial

component in the last phase of therapy. She acknowledged her wish for perfection ("It's stupid, but I keep thinking about how wrinkled my skin is and how fat my thighs are") and her fears of aging. The process for a woman of reclaiming her feminine beauty in an aging body is difficult and inspiring. Both the therapists and Larry were surprised at the degree and detail of Louise's self-hatred. Her strongly held inner convictions that she was fat and ugly were almost impenetrable to others' encouragement or praise. Finally, she was able to see this. By disclaiming all personal power concerning her appearance, she had bound others to praising and complimenting her repeatedly. Others' positive responses to her appearance were just a "drop in the bucket" of self-hatred, however, as she fiercely clung to a diminished image of herself. She had to give up, to simply stop saying that her aging body could not be "beautiful" or "powerful." Partly through looking at nude pictures of other women her age and through the empathy of the female therapist, Louise began to see her own body differently. In the end, she recovered some joy and pleasure in decorating herself and in understanding the expression of her unique personality in the contours and colors of her appearance.

Although we have reviewed some of the process of this last phase in working with couples, we have not given the whole picture, partly because we do not know it. The struggle to embrace the repressed feminine is ongoing and uncharted. In our work, we have come to believe that certain elements will typically be present during the phase of restoration of basic trust. In the man, we should see signs of acknowledging dependence, shame and anger, as well as a turning of strength and intelligence toward aspects of care-giving. In the woman, we should see some expressions of restored vitality, authority and self-worth. In her development, these autonomous strivings should be accompanied by learning how to trust others to provide care and encouragement. As she steps out of her bitter dependence and away from the projection of her autonomy needs, she will develop a realistic desire to become her own person and not blame her partner for her limitations. For both people, there should be an increasing understanding that the basis of empathy and trust is protecting the other's autonomy and honoring one's own. Acknowledging one's own limitations, vulnerabilities and imperfections is the foundation for accepting these human qualities in the other. Learning to value the undeveloped or weaker aspects of oneself is the basis for rejecting an illusory and severe "self-reliance." Our weaknesses and vulnerabilities can be supported and understood in a caring partnership when trust is well enough established and maintained.

The concern for reciprocal trust must be maintained on an every-day basis in couple relationships in middle and later life. Spending time together and sharing experiences are the only ways in which the trust can be supported. Just spending time is not the issue, of course, but it is the bottom-line requirement. During such times, the couple will discover the meanings buried in their unconscious com-munications and in their non-rational expressions. The regular ex-change of insights and images from dreams and fantasies, from fears and hurts, will become the basis for a deeper intuitive understanding of each others' psyches. Moving beyond the constraints of our habit-ual projections and the blaming of our partners for our own limita-tions is the ground for individuation in later life. Because we have so few models for the development of a truly shared bond of trust in adult relationships, we all need to search for the images which inspire us. Ragnell and Gawain can serve as guides for the establish-ment of mutual trust. The marriage begins at the end of the story.

to p. 140

6

Methodology in Couple Therapy

Two attitudes are especially helpful in doing psychotherapy with couples, *informed discovery* and *objective empathy.*

Informed discovery is an attitude of openness whereby the therapists bring conscious plans and ideas into the therapeutic relationship but hold them tentatively in a spirit of discovery. The emphasis should be on "conscious" because couple therapy requires a framework for management and direction of the work, as well as access to one's imagination in the moment. This is so because the complexity of the interpersonal field, which includes two members of a client couple and two members of a therapist couple, is greater than in individual, one-to-one therapy. Objective empathy is the ability of the therapist to understand and feel another person's experience accurately, as if it were the therapist's own, while keeping the *as if* in the foreground of awareness.

There is tension inherent in both of these attitudes. Informed discovery requires a tension between guiding concepts and responsive imagination. Objective empathy requires a tension between feeling intimately with the client and making objective assessments of what is taking place. (By objectivity, I do not mean a dualistic separation of the "object" from the "subject," but rather an attitude of mind that permits one to see through confusion to understanding, to see through the facts to the truth of the matter.)

Informed discovery develops from training in a number of therapeutic orientations and from one's own experience in therapy, both as client and therapist. Gathering and integrating useful concepts to illuminate the functioning of human personality and relationship become the foundation for expertise as a psychotherapist. From our experience, this means studying with others who have mastered both the "ideal" and the "real" of therapeutic practice. On the side of the ideal, one must be knowledgeable concerning theories and research on personality development, intrapsychic expressions and psychotherapy strategies and techniques. On the side of the real, one must learn how to practice psychotherapy, both through experience and through apprenticeship with more experienced practitioners. These two overlapping avenues of development as a therapist should come to include a wide range of different conceptual frameworks and modalities and be guided by one's own style or personality.

Students of psychology and psychotherapy need to be able to follow their own preferences in terms of their comfort and facility in using the techniques and theories available to them. When one has acquired a "critical mass" of this kind of learning, one feels more like a *person* acting in the role of therapist, more imaginatively available to one's self and more confident of one's actions as a responsible agent. Being guided by one's own preferences through the maze of different ideas and concepts about theory and practice will eventually result in feeling like a therapist while being a person (rather than feeling like a student while being a therapist).

After one has achieved this personal involvement in being a therapist, one can proceed with an attitude of informed discovery. Informed discovery is rooted in knowing one's concepts and techniques so well that they can be held very lightly in the face of new experience. We think that this is the attitude Jung recommended when he advised that analysts set aside their formal training and theory when they enter into a therapeutic relationship with an analysand. Far from approaching the therapeutic relationship without conceptual sets (an impossibility, of course), one approaches therapy with such a thorough integration of these sets into one's own vocabulary and actions that they seem quite natural and flexible. We have found that a good personal test of this is the therapist's ability to stand back from her or his professional orientation and see it humorously and imaginatively.

Objective empathy follows from informed discovery if one has come to understand one's own actions and thoughts thoroughly. As a result of personal psychotherapy, personal development and living fully (the process of individuation), the therapist comes to know the regions of human suffering within oneself. The combination of conscious objective plans or strategies with knowledge of oneself should result in an ability to see other people *as if* they were oneself. Objective empathy thus engenders both a compassionate closeness with another's suffering and the objective ability to see the suffering in context, as meaningful and growth-oriented.

Of course, the attitudes of informed discovery and objective empathy are themselves ideals. No one wholly realizes them—perhaps not even in a single therapeutic session—but they remain as guiding principles for being a useful therapist. As ideals or principles, they must be protected by ongoing personal development, consultation, training and education throughout one's practice as a therapist. In our experience as teachers and practitioners of psychotherapy, we have come to believe that no one ever attains security in the ability to maintain a general sense of objectivity, empathy and discovery without constantly working on oneself, especially on one's failures and blindspots.

Consequently, failures and blindspots guide our development as psychotherapists as they guide our development as persons. Being able to see a weakness, failure or the experience of despair as the key to further development is an essential contribution Jung has made to the practice of psychotherapy. His psychology, more than any other, emphasizes the idea that a deficit or weakness is not "just" a deficit or weakness. Failure provides insight for development, but it is not to be transformed too quickly. Rather, a tension is maintained between one's awareness of the potential for development in loss and the experience of loss itself.

With these general principles in mind, let us look at some of our specific guidelines for doing couple psychotherapy from a Jungian perspective.

Guidelines for Therapists

In our experience, therapists are strengthened by having partners to work with in couple therapy. Partly this is due to the complexity of the material which arises. In simple terms, two heads are better than one. When collaborating with a co-therapist, one can observe, interpret, and consult in the moment. Understanding the competing levels of reality in a couple relationship is difficult, even for two therapists, and can be overwhelming for one.

Although there are many arguments to support the greater coherence of strategy and technique that comes from having a single therapist, we believe that the benefits of collaborative therapy outweigh the deficits. Consequently, the framework we present in this chapter rests on the assumption that at least two therapists will be involved with the couple. We cannot claim that we are adequate to all of the levels of meaning which might evolve in the strategies and techniques we present. In the interest of simple language and a useful set of instructions, we will focus on the descriptive and talk about what can be seen in others and readily observed in oneself.

First of all choosing a partner for co-therapy is itself a complex task. The therapist couple is a reflection of the client couple on many levels of interaction. At the level of imitation or learning, the therapist couple should be able to demonstrate, in their actions and conversation, a sense of objective empathy with each other. They should also be able to demonstrate the modes of communication and interpretation they are attempting to engender in the couple. Furthermore, they should appear as "congruent experts," each having particular strengths and powers which seem to balance out equally in their partnership. Finally, they need to be perceived as individuals as well as partners, and not fused together as a symbiotic unit (e.g., finishing each others' sentences and thoughts). Working with a therapist partner involves the development of trust, mutuality and reciprocity in a couple relationship. Choosing a partner for this kind of development is not as important as choosing an intimate partner, as in marriage, but it is similar in its interpersonal demands.

One should be guided by one's own sense of comfort, respect and style in choosing a co-therapist. Working with a number of co-therapists before choosing is ideal. Finding out how one collaborates in sessions and how the rhythms of communication work with a co-therapist will contribute to one's ability to choose well. Many people do not have the luxury or freedom of this discovery, or even of a choice of co-therapist, especially in a clinic setting. When the freedom is available, however, it is wise to take advantage of it.

What are the guidelines, then? Find someone with whom you can communicate openly and clearly. This is the primary qualification for a co-therapist. If you cannot listen to each other reflectively and respond empathically, you will not be able to help others do so. Secondly, measure your own emotional comfort with the potential partner. If you are anxious or afraid, angry or submissive during most of your contacts with the other therapist, you will have the same feelings—and much exaggerated—doing therapy together. Finally, be certain that your theoretical and practical orientations "fit." This does not mean that both therapists must come from the same theoretical orientation (although this often helps), but that the orientations should be compatible. Ideally, the partners should be "optimally different" so that they can learn from each other. Optimal difference entails disparities in ideas and approaches that are just different enough not to provoke too much anxiety in each other, but to be a source of challenge and interest to each other.

Differences in sex, race, age and ethnic background of co-therapists are also important. There are no simple guidelines for these differences. You should feel like a couple—a couple of friends or a couple of intimates. From our experience, the feeling of being a couple comes from the dimension of partnership and sharing; there is a felt sense of companionship between the two people. Marriage partners may work well together as co-therapists or they may not. If the marriage relationship is relatively well individuated, such that the partners experience themselves as both autonomous and empathic, they are potentially good therapy partners. If the marriage partners are experiencing a lot of personal distress in their own relationship, however, this will necessarily emerge in their work in therapy. The distress can be helpful if it is optimally present, contributing to discovery and challenge, but not too much to anxiety. If the distress is too prominent, it will engender anxiety only. Similarly, same-sex couple relationships can be effective for co-therapy if the relationship is good enough. Great differences in age and ethnic or racial background are generally contraindicated for co-therapy. Because a lot of family-of-origin material is drawn out during therapy, great differences can contribute to very different assumptions. If these are not well worked through by the co-therapists, they can interfere with communication in sessions.

In addition to these interpersonal considerations in choosing a co-therapist, there are some significant professional ones. What kinds of couples and/or families do you want to work with? Nuclear families, extended families, gay families, cohabiting couples, single-parent families and blended families are just some of the family and couple configurations you can meet. Overall, it is advisable that the therapists have had experience in being in the kind of couple or family arrangement they are treating. Personal prejudices and unexamined assumptions certainly interfere with effectiveness in couple therapy. For example, working with a gay mother and her lover should involve some acquaintance with such a couple's assumptions and lifestyles if one is to be effective in clarifying communication patterns and helping the partners change their actions. When you are choosing your co-therapist, then, you must keep in mind the kinds of couples the two of you can reflect. Do not attempt to treat those people toward whom you feel judgmental, uninformed or overwhelmed. A good rule of thumb is to specialize, to some extent, in helping couples that are familiar to you in your own couple relationships. The dynamics constellated in the therapist couple will affect the dynamics which emerge in therapy and which orient the therapists in their interventions. In choosing a co-therapist, then, one should have in mind some "population" or lifestyles for which the therapist couple can be effective psychotherapists.

Finally, the therapist partners need time to relate to each other both before and after sessions. We allow a half hour before and an hour after to work through our ideas, feelings, plans and evaluations. Since we advocate generally that a session be two hours in length, this means allowing three and a half hours for working with each couple.

Naturally, the element of time interfaces with money. Co-therapists will generally have to charge more for their work than will single therapists. Since it is impossible to measure the "worth" of two therapists versus one therapist, the problem of fees requires constant communication, and even consultation, with other therapists. Balancing considerations of the "going rate," the ability of your clients to pay, the number of sessions (and their timing) that you recommend, both of your financial needs, and your own complexes involving money will be an ongoing interactive process. Similarly, which of you will receive the actual payment, how you will collect the fees and how you will evaluate the worth of your services will be ongoing matters of discussion. If you cannot discuss money with a potential co-therapist, you will not be suitable partners.

If you are in a situation such as a clinic or graduate program in which you have no opportunity to choose a co-therapist, you need to be aware of the dimensions that will be problematic at the outset. When working with an unknown or assigned co-therapist, do not anticipate a true partnership or necessarily effective therapy sessions. Since partnership in co-therapy is a personal, even intimate matter, you cannot evaluate the effectiveness of co-therapy from experiences with people you do not know. When working with an assigned co-therapist, the best guideline for effectiveness is to pay attention to the unspoken dimensions of communication and take plenty of time before and after the sessions to discuss your work. If this time is not available, anticipate a great deal of frustration and try not to "act out" the frustration during the therapy session. Consultation and supervision may be the only opportunities you have for exploring your relationship with the co-therapist. Take advantage of these occasions because the relationship with the co-therapist is as important as what is done and said in the therapeutic session itself. In my clinical teaching and supervision, I have often encountered situations in which the student and "expert" co-therapist actually played out the problems of their own relationship instead of focusing on what the couple presented.

It is my strong belief, from my experience in practicing and teaching, that the direction of the therapeutic interaction is influenced more by the "charged" elements of the therapists than by those of the clients when the therapists are unconscious of those elements. Charged elements are those emotional expressions which constellate archetypal complexes in an interpersonal field. Because the clients anticipate expertise in the therapists, clients are more readily guided by the therapists' interests and questions than by their own. When co-therapists are angry, power-struggling and confused partners, they will tend to energize the interpersonal field with their own struggles. Clients will initially cooperate because their role is to be more submissive, because they are in need and because they are uninformed or unassertive about what kind of help they should be getting. If this kind of interference from the therapist couple occurs too often, clients will not return because they will not experience themselves as being helped. Of course, this is not the only reason why clients do not return, but it is an important reason. In co-therapy, the opportunity for the therapist couple to constellate complexes of their own is perhaps greater than in individual therapy, in which the client and therapist must constellate together.

Occasionally videotaping yourselves as co-therapists will contribute greatly to your ability to help couples. Video and audiotaping, while they interfere with the privacy of psychotherapy, are necessary to the learning process in co-therapy. The co-therapist partners can understand better their continuing thematic contributions to the interpersonal field when they see these in context with different couples. Seeing other co-therapists work together also contributes to understanding your own idiosyncracies, especially in the realm of gestures, manner of speech and other expressions of non-rational complexes.

Finally, a few reminders about the interactive field within the therapist couple's relationship. I prefer to speak of an interactive field in psychotherapy, in general, rather than in terms of transference and countertransference. (At best, we are unclear about how to separate out these contributing factors in the interpersonal field; at worst, we tend to think dualistically in terms of "placing blame" on one or the other contributor to the field.) Naturally, the therapist couple will find constellated the same kinds of non-rational complexes that they find in other intimate relationships. Mother, father and god complexes are most frequently constellated, with occasional child complexes traipsing along. From watching videotapes and working with a variety of couples, you will come to know the complexes which you most frequently constellate in your own couple relationship in therapy. You can use these in the kinds of creative, active interventions we will be describing (e.g., role reversal) and can learn to anticipate them as familiar companions in the therapeutic work. If you find that you constellate very troubling negative complexes, such as the frequently observed negative mother complex, you should seek some consultation on your work. By tracing out your family-of-origin messages and interactive patterns which contribute to your complexes, and by "hearing the complexes speak" in the moment, you can discover what is creative and useful in the non-rational field between you. Moreover, you can learn to avoid what is not useful.

Because complexes are out of one's intentional control, the best the therapist couple can do when their complex is "running" a session negatively is back off and let the client couple do the interacting for a while. As will be explained below, therapists can direct the clients to talk about a topic while the therapists listen, or they can direct the clients to carry out an activity while the therapists observe. This kind of client interaction can provide a breather in a session in which the therapist couple's complexes have become confusing or otherwise disruptive. Through experience and training, you will come to know, as certain topics arise, what complexes are typically constellated between you and your partner, and you will learn how to use these constructively within the therapeutic session.

Initial Contact with Clients

Clients reach us through referral, through direct contact or through selecting us impersonally from some source like the telephone book. We need some method of quickly assessing the kind of family, couple and individuals we are dealing with. We also have an advance agreement, between ourselves, about whom we will treat and whom we will refer.

We find that we do our best work with couples who seek our help after hearing us in a public lecture or being referred by friends who have heard us present our orientation. These people generally let us know, over the telephone, that they know about our work and are motivated, within themselves, to seek our help. Typically, the woman of a heterosexual couple makes the contact and sets up the first interview. With a "familiar" couple like this, we are primed to think in terms of our entire program of intervention, as described below. Usually, we are contacted by couples in middle life or by feminist-oriented heterosexual couples when we are sought by those familiar with our work.

The couples who are unfamiliar present a different problem, which becomes the focus of our attention in the initial assessment: is the couple enough like us to benefit from our interventions? In the initial telephone contact, we ask a couple how they found out about our work. When the caller is unfamiliar with us as Jungian or feminist therapists, we make a note that we will need to assess the couple before we proceed.

Our concerns focus mostly on the couple's capacity to use interventions that entail the ability to be reflective and imaginative. If either one or both members of the couple would find this kind of work totally unfamiliar, troubling or thoroughly beyond their usual means of relating and expressing, we have to consider our realistic capacity to help the couple.

Next, our concerns focus on the presenting problem. Sometimes the caller presents the problem on the telephone as though the problem were actually the partner's; a caller may say, for example, "I would like to get some help for my husband in therapy, and because he won't go by himself, I will come along." Clarification of the presenting problem is important even at this early stage. We will say, "If you believe that your husband needs individual therapy or counseling, talk with him about it and have him call for an individual appointment." We stress, even at this stage, the idea that the couple is interacting in the problem, if indeed it is a problem concerning the couple. Another way a couple seeks therapy is when children "refer" their parents for therapy by expressing the parents' struggling through school failures or social misdemeanors. Many couples have been referred to us through school counselors because their children are in trouble. In this kind of case, we ask the parents to come in order to "talk about what has been happening with your daughter/son."

In the initial session with a couple, our opening procedure is to have the couple sit facing one another, while we are seated in chairs which are slightly behind and to the side of each partner. We open the session by saying, "We would like you to talk with each other, just as you might have done in the car coming here, about what you want from being here." If a particular problem has already been mentioned, then we ask them to talk about it—e.g., "We would like you to talk about your impressions of the problems your daughter is having at school." We stress that they are to look at each other and talk together while we listen. We are each seated outside of one partner's field of vision, and we focus our eyes on something other than the face of the other partner. Some people find our procedure anxiety-provoking because we observe no social niceties within the consulting room (we always shake hands in greeting the couple in the waiting room and offer them tea or coffee if they desire). We notice how they handle both the ambiguity and the exposure of this initial situation. Our interest is in evaluating their suitability for the kind of work we usually do with couples.

We ask ourselves the following kinds of questions:

1) How anxious are they about talking in front of us and about having one therapist out of the visual field (e.g., how often does that person turn around to look at the therapist who is out of view)?

2) How comfortable are they with talking to each other? Eye contact, familiarity, gestures and general sense of "helpfulness" to each other?

3) How much do they need our approval to continue?

4) Are they motivated by their own energies—anger, sadness,

hurt, etc.—to change things in their relationship?

5) What is their level of expressed aggression or hostility?

6) How easy are they in translating back and forth from meta-phoric to literal meaning?

In order to do the kind of therapy we describe here, we look for evidence of the couple's ability to sustain themselves in an ambiguous and anxiety-provoking environment. In general, we find them more promising if we get some emotional cue—either through their expression or through our felt experience—of anger, hurt, resentment, bitterness, despair or depression. These emotions will be motivators initially. On the other hand, if much expressed or unexpressed rage, hostility or aggression is picked up at this point (typically coming from men who are abusive either physically or emotionally), the couple is not a good candidate for the provocative kinds of techniques we will use.

The partners should also be self-sustaining enough in their relationship to have some brief conversation without looking for our approval too often. If they speak only a word or two and then say, "What do you want us to do now?", they are not good candidates for developing their own interpersonal arena, the kind we will need for therapy. Finally, if they seem not to be able to speak with some natural metaphorical allusions, but use only impoverished adjectives like "nice," "okay" and literal descriptions, it is unlikely that they will understand interventions which involve symbolic reality.

After about five or ten minutes of allowing them to talk, the co-therapists engage in a dialogue of their own about what they have heard. If the client couple seems suitable for our Jungian, active approach, we immediately talk in terms of the complexes we have observed. We do not use the word "complex," but describe the interactive field in terms which lead us toward the negative mother complex, that is, the hero, bully or the hag. For example, we might say, "Louise seems to feel that Larry doesn't understand her at all. She has almost given up on using words to describe what she feels. I think she has lost faith in the relationship altogether because she has been in pain for so long." Or we might say, "Larry is a very rational person who likes to solve problems even before understanding them." Besides characterizing their identity states, we may also speak about their projections in terms of what they seem to need and to fear in each other. We may also allude to unspoken emotions such as, "I think both of them are quite angry, but not able to express their anger openly." We try to pull out the emotions of hurt, resentment, fear, anger and despair that have been hidden and that will help us in working with them. Also, whenever possible, we attempt to use some appropriate light humor such as, "I thought Larry was about to leave the room, he pulled his chair so far away from Louise." We are interested in their ability to see themselves objectively and to laugh at their exaggerations.

If the couple seems not suited for our kind of work, we will do one of several things. One of us may tell the other co-therapist that one of the individuals needs separate treatment at the moment: "I think I will ask Louise a few questions while you and Larry just watch." Or we will say to each other that we should each interview the partner of our own sex in order to explore things privately: "Let's talk to Larry and Louise separately for a while and get to know each of them." If we believe that they are not at all suitable for any kind of couple therapy, we will indicate then and there that we would like to pursue individual therapy, or we will take some other route—referral to a group, for example. (More detailed information about this procedure will follow in the next chapter.)

If we decide to proceed with our usual format, we pull our chairs into a circle with the couple and spend a few minutes talking with them about the initial assessment experience. We are interested in their reactions to the observations we have made about them and in their reactions to the "exposure" of talking in front of us. Usually we don't have to invite them to speak; simply by pulling our chairs up, we signal that they can talk and they do. Because we have just begun our assessment process, we do not want them to respond too much at this time, and we try to limit their initial comments and our responses to a maximum of five minutes.

If the woman is very tearful at this point, she may need separate attention before we proceed. Primarily she will need empathic support because she is experiencing despair. Because we generally attune ourselves immediately to the most painful meanings and feelings between them, we will have heightened their suffering rather than diminished it. Sometimes we are also depressed at this point ourselves and need to gesture support to each other. In extreme situations, we may leave the room for a brief consultation in which we try immediately to get a context for what is happening. (For example, we may ask each other questions about unfinished grieving, possible physical abuse, secret lovers and the like.)

Assessment of the Interpersonal Field

Most of the initial session is assessment for us, but we do use various techniques immediately. Simply by talking about our reflections in front of the couple, we are creating a context for open communication, especially about the non-rational elements of the interpersonal field (hereafter also referred to as "the field"). Usually we do not understand what is really going on in the field until our own wrap-up session afterward. We use a number of activities to assess the complexes which are generated in the field, the areas of competence and vulnerability of the individuals, and the ongoing life context of their everyday environment (especially the stresses in it).

We often use a short exercise which I learned as a student from Professor Thomas Allen of Washington University in St. Louis.[1] It permits us quickly to assess how accurate the partners are in empathizing with each other and how each individual conceptualizes the field between them.

Interpersonal Assessment:
One therapist introduces the exercise by giving the following instructions more or less verbatim:

We would like to ask you a few questions to which you will write brief answers. Your answers will help us understand more about what brings you here. There are no right or wrong answers to our questions, and we would like you to be as frank as possible. Here is a pad on which to write your answers. Put your first name in the upper-right corner.

The first question: On a scale from 0 to 10, rank your need for this relationship. At the low end, a 0 would mean that you hardly need the relationship at all and that you consider yourself entirely independent of it most of the time. On the high end, 10 would indicate that the relationship is as necessary as the air you breathe for your well-being. Number your answer #1 and answer now.

The second question, numbered 2: What is the greatest problem in your relationship, from your own point of view, right now as you sit here? (They should be given the time they each need to answer.)

The third question, numbered 3: What is the greatest satisfaction in your relationship, from your perspective, right now? What do you value most about this relationship?

The fourth question, numbered 4, is a little different from the others: Write down the number you think your partner gave to the first question. What did your partner give as the ranked importance of this relationship in her/his life?

The fifth question: What did your partner say is the most difficult problem in your relationship at this time? (Often this takes more time than the others.)

The sixth question: What does your partner think is the greatest reward in this relationship at this time?

When the partners have finished the exercise, we take the pads and look over their answers. Usually we begin the unraveling of these answers with something that is likely to provoke anxiety. For example, with a couple we once saw, the man rated their relationship as of 0 importance to him while the wife had given its importance to her a 9. We began by asking the woman to ask her husband how he rated the relationship and then to share with him what she had thought (a 7). The brief answers generate a lot of information, so we usually stay with this sharing exercise until each of them has expressed what was written. Sometimes we help the couple explore some dimension of what has been mentioned by using the technique of "doubling" (explained below), whereby the therapists act as alter-ego voices for each member of the couple.

After exploring this exercise, my co-therapist and I take a five-minute break during which we plan what our next steps will be. Typically, we begin one of the intervention techniques described below to explore further the hurt, anger and resentment. Our goal is to "dig around" in the hurt enough so that all of us can feel the potential loss of the relationship very directly.

Assessing the complex has three dimensions: 1) confrontation with loss, 2) mapping the non-rational expressions and 3) uncovering secrets.

In confronting loss, we want to experience empathically the couple's sense of potential loss. We will explore topics like the length of their commitment, children, homelife, established shared interests and social networks, extended family, their early romance ("Describe the person you fell in love with twenty years ago") and their intimate sex life. Generally the couple's sex life is non-existent or barely surviving. We also ask about financial dependence (sometimes money is the woman's answer to the question about the greatest benefit for her in the relationship), career commitments and future work plans. At this stage, we are usually supporting the hag's voice, which despairs about any goodness in any of the life they have built together. By empathizing with the voice, we strengthen the woman's experience that she might have a legitimate perspective on the pain of life "out in the woods." We are interested to discover how difficult or easy it is for her to formulate an autonomous position. From this we can tell whether she is an early or later Ragnell: whether she has become habituated to being isolated and will need much help in "coming out," or whether she is close to saying, "I have the answer."

Similarly, for the man, we want to find out how much he has compensated for the loss in his experience and/or how much he has come to behave aggressively or dominantly to obtain his own way. The issue of physical abuse of children or partner can enter into our exploration of the bully role. If we intuit that abuse might be happening, we do everything we can to bring it out into the open. It is essential to do this in an atmosphere of "no blame," by empathizing with the man's despair and anger.

Mapping non-rational expressions entails noting the kinds of gestures and implied meanings that each partner uses to express unarticulated feelings in the complex. For example, one woman always went into her bedroom, shut the door and cried when she was furious with her husband. We reframed this activity as an expression of anger. During our sessions with this couple, we were gradually able to teach the wife some words for her anger, even though she continued to express it mostly through withdrawal. We could understand her withdrawal as anger, and her husband eventually became able to respond appropriately to her anger by creating the boundaries between his son and himself that were appropriately desired by his wife. As we observe implied meanings in archetypal facial expressions, gestures and images, we use words to name the feeling states expressed. We may follow a gesture back to its family-of-origin meaning and define it in imagistic terms. For example, a particular nodding of the head in one man was reminiscent of the passive-aggression of his grandfather. When the man nodded his head in this way, one of us would say, "Well, I guess that Grandpa Smith is present—I wonder how he got in."

In this initial session, we are simply discovering and labeling the archetypal behaviors that express basic human emotions, especially those which have been denied or hidden by the couple.

Finally, we want to assess the "secret spells" that are contained in the couple's hidden contracts or unspoken agreements. Carl Sager's work in this area has been helpful to us.[2] Usually when partners enter into a relationship, they have an unspoken contract which allows each individual to satisfy her or his needs. For instance, the contract may be for the woman to provide housekeeping and child-care in exchange for the man's provision of financial support and rational guidance for the family. Usually sexual monogamy is part of the couple's contract. Sub-contracts within the overall agreement indicate other hidden concerns such as who will initiate sex, what sexual freedoms each partner has, who will manage the money and so on. Although these contracts are not explicitly verbalized, they are important in maintaining agreement and trust between partners. When basic trust has broken down, the initial contract has always been violated—by one or both partners. A typical situation is that the initial contract was never replaced by another agreement that was mutually satisfying, so both partners are angry and hurt. Our short written exercise gives us clues as to what remains and what has been violated in the contract. The assumptions and projections made by each partner will also give clues as to the original contract and its violation.

In many middle life couples, the first breaking of the contract was initiated by the woman in her refusal to be a servant in some regard. Either she freed herself for school, stopped doing housework or satisfied her emotional needs with a lover. Through her behavior, she said "No" to the original agreement that she would be dominated by her husband's needs. However, she did nothing to substitute for the tasks that she abandoned. Although the husband may not consciously know that he is furious in response to her breaking her part of the "bargain," he may have enacted a betrayal scene in response to his wife's behavior.

When either one or both partners has an outside lover, their distress about the breakdown of trust can be obscured. In our search for any hidden dimensions of the original dominance-submission spell, we look especially at the husband's rational tolerance of what he apparently dislikes in his wife's independence (expressed in her refusals to cooperate). Sometimes, holding a separate interview with each partner is the only way to discover their secrets. Often, however, the secrets just break through on their own in the couple's dialogue.

In an atmosphere of "no blame," we encourage the speaking of secrets. Once we have intuited or otherwise discovered a secret that is being kept from one partner (usually involving sexual or financial betrayal), we do everything we can to encourage the secret to come forth—everything short of revealing it ourselves. Talking about the "magic binding" power of secrets to isolate the partners from each other and the helpfulness of revealing secrets is one method that frequently works. Revealing some hidden or secret aspects of our own momentary therapeutic interactions can create an openness that the couple will imitate. At the very least, we state that secrets in the area of their relationship contract will definitely interfere with our ability to help them revitalize the relationship. Often we describe basic trust as a flame which can die out if it does not have proper tending and adequate fuel and air. Secrets tend to stifle the flame.

Of course, we expect that each member of the couple will have a private life as well as a life as part of a couple, so we do not advocate the revealing of all of an individual's private life. It is only in the area of hurtful secrets which obscure the person's commitment to partnership in intimacy that we encourage the revealing of secrets.

One way or another, we take a strong position regarding the

necessity of a monogamous commitment to relationship throughout the process of therapy. We believe that the couple relationship, rather than the client-therapist relationship, is the interactive field which frames therapy with couples. When sexual or intimate emotional needs are being met by someone outside the couple, then the work of therapy can be dissipated or drained off by the outside arrangements. We make a statement in this regard if we suspect or know that either one or both partners is sexually or emotionally betraying the other.

In the final fifteen or so minutes of our initial session, the co-therapists talk together, in front of the client couple, about their assessment of the interpersonal field, emphasizing themes from each of the areas we have mentioned. In addition to emphasizing potential loss, we speak about the hopeful aspects, the strengths of the individuals and their foundation of commitment to each other. We are supportive of the woman's pain and the reality of her isolation and struggle. We are equally supportive of the man's tolerance and the reality of his responsibilities and isolation. Usually both partners have opened up by this time and are identifying positively with the reflections of the therapists. We always assign some homework task during this time, something that the couple will be responsible for carrying out on their own in the interval between sessions. If this is a single session for assessment purposes, then we suggest tasks that might help them in the future.

The Therapeutic Contract

At the end of the assessment, we identify particular goals based on what we have understood in the initial session. The goals are as concrete and behavior-oriented as possible, and they respond to the initial presenting problem of the couple. We may talk in terms of improving non-rational communications, clarifying these and translating some of them into words. We may speak about the "ordinary tasks of living" and the sharing of household and care-giving roles. We often formulate a goal that directs the couple toward greater intimacy and shared time. When a child or children are involved in the presenting problem, we formulate our goals in such a way as to respond to this initial concern. At the very least, we reframe the "problem child" as a "problem in the couple relationship." Or we may integrate activities concerning the child into the goals. We may state that we will eventually see them with their child or children, but typically we will not plan to see any children until the final session or two.

For most couples we set up five two-hour therapy sessions following the initial interview. The sessions are each a month apart. A seventh, or follow-up session, is planned to take place six months after the last of the five regular sessions. We explain that the major work of the therapy takes place outside, in their relationship, and that we are simply consultants in this process. If they have problems carrying out their homework assignments, they are to telephone us rather than drop the assignment. If they have an emergency for which they need to see us between our regular sessions, they can call for a special appointment. We also tell them that they are to pay us immediately after each session (we have told them our fee over the telephone).

Strategies and Techniques

The following strategies are basic principles of psychotherapy which hold for most therapies and extend across theoretical schools. Each of these strategies is enacted within the special framework of a therapeutic relationship. They characterize the ways in which psychotherapy is a unique interpersonal relationship that can be readily distinguished from other intimate relationships. They were mentioned and briefly explained in chapter two: 1) management of the therapeutic relationship, 2) meaning reconstruction, 3) new learning and 4) expansion of vocabulary for meaning making.

I consider these strategies basic to any practice of therapy that is called "psychotherapy." They all contribute to helping people change their conscious attitudes, their lifestyles and their habitual actions and thoughts. They are used in individual, couple, family and group psychotherapies which use different techniques. In discussing each of these strategies in terms of Jungian psychotherapy with couples, I will describe some of the relational features involved in the strategy and then describe one or two techniques we use in carrying out the strategy. A technique is a particular intervention; it is easily described, and more observable than the strategy itself is. Some of the active techniques we use derive from psychodrama, while the interpretive techniques derive from Jungian psychology. The behavioral techniques come from behavior therapy. We find that this combination of active and interpretive interventions is especially effective and dramatic in working with couples.

Management of the Therapeutic Relationship

The therapeutic relationship is the interactive field in which the therapy takes place. From our perspective, it is a field broadly characterized by basic trust or rapport between members. In individual therapy, this rapport (often called "positive transference" or "therapeutic alliance") is established over a rather long period of time. Until it is established, the therapeutic field will commonly consist of what William Goodheart has called the "persona-restoring" aspects of relating.[3] Both people will retreat behind the persona: the therapist into the activities of "expert," and the client into activities of "regular person" or "sufferer" or whatever. Until rapport is established, little collaborative and mutual work will be accomplished.

In couple therapy, the rapport is already established between the members of the couple, although it may be somewhat damaged at the time therapy begins. The anxiety and stress of the actual therapeutic session will tend to restore the couple's rapport and bind them as a unit (unless they are ready to separate). It is this unit of the couple relationship which is the primary field to be mapped in couple therapy. The co-therapists have their own rapport and are somewhat outside of the therapeutic relationship of the couple.

In order to be believed as experts or authorities, the therapists must appear to know what they are doing in managing the session. Although they may join temporarily in rapport with one or both members of the couple, they enter the field as experts. Management of the therapeutic field in couple and family work requires acting as an authority and directing the action within the couple relationship. This is a quite different experience from building rapport and using it within individual therapy. Some people find this kind of manager's or consultant's role less appealing and more anxiety-provoking than others do. Because the co-therapists experience the client relationship as "formed" and somewhat resistant to outsiders, they will use various techniques in order to affect it. A technique which we use in a variety of ways to put pressure on the therapeutic field within the session is what we call an *empathy interview.*

Empathy Interview: Choose a charged or difficult topic (e.g., distrust about money) and interview the more affected member of the couple. Usually the interview works best with the co-therapist of the same sex as the client. The other co-therapist and client pull back their chairs and watch the interview in silence.

This interview should follow basic rules for empathic understanding:

a) Facilitate rapport between therapist and client by establishing a shared sense of mutuality (e.g., we both "understand" such and such). Mediate the rapport by applying pressure for greater exploration of the difficult topic.

b) Facilitate greater understanding of the topic by reformulating its meaning along some new symbolic or interpersonal line. For example, reformulate an act of withdrawal as an assertive act of anger.

c) Use reflective listening and responses to increase the affective experience of the client.

d) Integrate archetype as such (gestural), archetypal complex (implied meaning) and expressed personal reality whenever possible. This retrieval of various levels of meaning should be congruent with the experience of the client.

When the interview has ended (it usually takes ten to fifteen minutes), the observers turn to each other and the other co-therapist asks the client partner, "What did you feel or observe as you were watching?" The material provided by the interview should expand a partner's ability to empathize with the other partner. Furthermore, it may open avenues to greater exploration of the feeling levels of the complex being examined. (The charged topic will inevitably be connected with a complex.)

Empathic listening and exploratory responses from the therapists will increase their ability to affect the couple relationship and to apply pressure in assigning tasks and directing the sessions.

Through the attitude of objective empathy, the therapists convey a felt understanding of the couple's problems and their position outside the problematic arena. More than in individual work, couple therapy exposes the therapist to enacting the role of an expert and can therefore constellate a parental or god complex. Empathic techniques help the therapists feel joined with clients and simply human. Empathy from therapists also allows the couple to feel comfortable and accurately reflected.

The balance of empathy and objectivity is especially important in managing the interactive field of the couple, for many directives are given by therapists in couple work. The directives include telling the clients where to sit, when to change perspective in the session, how to look or speak to each other and what assignments to do after the session. They do not typically involve advice-giving. Directives from the therapists should focus more on creating contexts, both in and out of the sessions, in which the partners can further their development. On the other hand, advice may be necessary if danger or abuse is involved—if, for example, the clients pose danger to themselves or to dependent others. We give advice about child management, the management of addictions (e.g., "Join AA") and "containing" aggressive hostility, when necessary. We do not give advice, however, unless there is the potential of personal or interpersonal danger.

Management of the therapeutic relationship focuses primarily, then, on the therapists' creating appropriate contexts and moving people and complexes in and out of the interactive field of the couple relationship. Management also involves securing the frame around the couple relationship by telling them they must be intimately committed to each other throughout the six-month period of active therapeutic intervention. If the therapy has worked, then basic trust and vitality are re-established and we find the couple continuing their commitment at the six-month follow-up interview.

Meaning Reconstruction

The strategy of meaning reconstruction involves the reworking of the conscious and unconscious paradigm the couple brings to the therapeutic encounter. This means helping the partners change their assumptions, expectations, projections and fantasies about each other so that they can relate more effectively as "ordinary persons." In Jungian terms, we assist them in distinguishing between archetypal and personal reality and help them to claim personal reality. The ideal is allowing each person to establish an inner dialectic of these realities for meaning making so that she or he attains ready access to personal responses and to archetypal imagination.

When a couple has severed the bond of basic trust, usually both members have been projecting archetypal complexes onto each other and have been limiting the personal responses that can occur between them. Rather than being able to see and experience the other as a person with an individual identity and appropriately limited personal responsibility for life, the partners experience each other as "gods" or "goddesses." Carrying the projection of hag or hero is exhausting to one's personal identity and sense of agency. Furthermore, when the projection is internalized and carried out as an identity state, it interferes with individuation.

By distinguishing between archetypal and personal reality and establishing an inner dialectic between the two, each person becomes able to continue developing. In part, this means that each individual carries more of the responsibility (sometimes felt initially to be a "burden") of her or his own development. For a couple, the dialectical stance also means that each partner can urge or encourage the other's development, now knowing that the other has the choice to pursue or not to pursue the urging.

The habitual projection of the woman's animus onto her husband, for example, decreases the possibility that she will develop her own authority and increases the possibility that she will be inaccurate in her ability to encourage her husband's personal development.

We typically find that the woman's animus projection onto her partner has elements of her father complex and her mother's animus. Often these unconscious elements are incongruent with the husband's real abilities and motivations, or at least with his personal style. Naturally something "hooks" the projection initially, but usually that hook is only part of the husband's repertoire of behavior.

To give a very specific example, one woman assumed that her bright and well-educated professional husband would "make a lot of money someday," and began their marriage unconsciously expecting that they would eventually live the "good life" that she had been accustomed to through her father's high earnings. When they entered marriage, they were both "hippie types" and the woman's unacknowledged desire for material possessions was neither in her conscious awareness nor displayed in her persona. After a few years during which the husband did charitable and valuable professional work, she began to egg him on to make more money. Although he had some hidden material desires himself, they were not at all as grand as those of his wife. By learning to discriminate her father complex from her husband, the woman became able to choose whether or not *she* wanted to make the additional money necessary for the lifestyle she desired.

The withdrawal and integration of the animus and anima complexes in the partners permits greater personal freedom for each. They should show evidence, in their daily behavior, of the kinds of changes in personality that indicate integration of these complexes. In the man, we typically find that the anima complex has been projected onto his wife in terms of her meeting or not being capable of meeting his fantasy of a "completely available" woman. Either he has decided that she is capable of meeting these impossible emotional needs and is angry because she "must be withholding," or he has decided that she is simply "not capable" of being the available woman and has selected other women for his projection. Also, he is usually convinced that his wife's emotions are "overwhelming and impossible." She is just "too emotional"—too depressed, too angry or too resentful, etc.—to be affected by his support or involvement. In fact, he is taking little responsibility for providing any nurturance for his wife, assuming that she should nurture herself and others around her. By integrating his own anima, he will become empathically involved with the emotional needs of his family and will begin to show that he truly understands what others want when they ask him for intimate involvement. His integration of his anima should be evidenced both in his appropriate emotional responsiveness in the sessions (different from overwhelming "anima moods") and from his taking on responsibility for care-giving at home.

A useful technique for encouraging the differentiation and integration of animus and anima complexes is a psychodrama intervention called *doubling*.

Doubling: The co-therapists act as alter egos for the client partners. This can take any form—e.g., each co-therapist doubling either partner—but typically takes the form of the same-sexed co-therapist doubling for that partner.

Arrange the chairs so that the alter-ego therapist is out of the field of vision of the client-speaker. Usually it is most effective for the therapist to sit just behind the left shoulder of the client being doubled. Clients face each other squarely.

The following kinds of instructions are given by one of the co-therapists: "We are going to help you communicate with each other more openly. Each of us will speak out of the felt experience which is unexpressed in each of you. We will speak as if we were you. When I speak for you, Larry, I will say things that I experience you feeling or thinking but not saying. Listen to what I say and if I am wrong, change the words or tell me. If I am accurate, then let Louise respond as if it were you speaking. Then just carry on from there. I would like you to elaborate, in your own words, what I have opened up—if it feels right. If we get into a problem, you can consult with me. I am a sort of alter ego or internal voice for you here, but I am also your partner and we may need to consult occasionally. My partner will do the same for Louise. Do you understand?"

Let the couple begin the dialogue. As soon as the complex is apparent, the therapists formulate words to express its underlying meaning. The words should be close to the client's language and generally be feeling statements. For example, the client says, "Maybe we should just make a decision to go away together for a weekend and get to know each other again." The therapist says, "I need to hold you and feel your love." The therapist emphasizes the direct unexpressed emotions. Depending on the stage of the therapy, the therapist may want to emphasize feelings of hurt, anger and depression/despair, or feelings of joy, love, satisfaction and pleasure.

Because the therapists are more informed than the couple about the bully, hag and hero roles in the negative mother complex, the therapist should be a "jump ahead" of the couple in understanding what is being implied.

After this kind of doubling has gone on for about fifteen or twenty minutes, the co-therapists join the couple in a circle and interpret what has happened, with their help.

Doubling inevitably leads to the technique of *interpretation*. We find that non-reductive interpretation (archetypal meanings) is usually more useful than reductive interpretation (family-of-origin patterns).

Non-reductive interpretation, because it calls on symbolic images and expressions from myth and stories, allows us to reveal meaning without blame. When we talk about the meaning of the hag or hero role, we speak about the typical demands of intimate adult bonding rather than the specific influences of one's own parents and early upbringing. Since the members of the couple have generally fought a great deal about each others' families, we can reframe this conflict as "typical" or simply expectable human life. We distinguish between the emotional reality of feeling compelled or driven by an inner state and the rational reality of making choices and being logical. Stressing the importance of listening and understanding the emotional as well as the rational, we discuss the personal responsibility for enacting the emotional aspects of relationship. Making impossible demands on others, in terms of one's own fantasies or ideals, can interfere with interpersonal satisfaction. Fantasies and ideals can also motivate us to expand our awareness when we take personal responsibility for them.

In this kind of non-reductive interpretation, we focus on the current conscious attitude and choose illustrations from what is happening in the room. For example, one man attacked me very angrily after I had doubled his wife, and he told all of us that I was "causing trouble and stirring up feelings" that his wife had never expressed. In responding, I told him that his angry feelings were misdirected at me and that I could see how frightened he was of the responsibility for his wife's hurt. I also told him that being a bully with his temper would usually frighten other people and make them back away from him. I went on to say that probably he felt afraid and lonely when he exploded like this and found himself isolated from others. In therapy, I did not find his anger overwhelming, but I experienced it as his own inherent energy, potentially available to him to enact the goals he admired but had not pursued. I said he was clearly a powerful person in taking command of our session, and that he could rely on this power in other situations, when he understood it.

Reductive interpretation, explaining current behavior in terms of past familial or social influences, is useful when the particular gestures and moods evoke fears of repeating the past. Rather than initiating this type of interpretation, we draw on what the couple brings up. One or both partners may indicate, for instance, that something is "just like your parents," or say hopelessly that they see themselves locked into the same battles their own parents had. We explore this arena of the family-of-origin in terms of gestures or implied symbolic meaning in the moment. If, for example, the client says, "Mother always got sick and went to bed when she was mad at us," we may say, "Now you have invited mother into the room. What did you want to do with her?" Generally we try to free the couple from the past in two ways. We show them that their parents were of a different generation, not as conscious and not as free to be individuals as the present couple is. (Whether or not this is true, it sets the stage. Often I use a version of a famous George Santayana quote, "Those who do not read history are condemned to repeat it," and tell the couple that we are learning to "read history" and therefore be free of it.) We also explain the difference between having a contextual understanding of an early life situation and simply acting it out. We encourage humor and imagination in responding to family-of-origin patterns.

Most of all, we make a distinction between the felt reality of archetypal complexes and the personal reality of what "really happened." The internalized mother or father complex, while it may be similar to some features of the people who parented us, is not the same as those people. The contemporary concerns and problems connected to parental complexes must be differentiated from the real parents. For some people, returning to the real parents—asking questions and gathering information—is a useful way to separate out the complexes and the people. For others, either this is an impossibility or creates greater confusion. From a Jungian perspective, it is especially important that we help people distinguish between these realities rather than further obscure their similarities and differences. Many approaches to family therapy encourage an investigation of extended family patterns as they operate in the present, without adequately differentiating between the parental complexes and the people involved in parenting roles.

Complexes are collections of images, feelings, experiences and habitual actions which are amassed around archetypal images. A complex results from experiences with many people, not simply with one or two. While a woman may be much influenced by her own mother's depression and lack of individual motivation, she has to have experienced the same thing in many other women—and in herself—if she is burdened with a weak and depressed mother complex in middle life. Talking with her own mother will not undo the projection of this complex onto her mother. Charting the complex, through her own therapy and her relationships, will assist her in understanding its meaning and withdrawing its projection onto current significant others. In using reductive interpretation, we must be alert to speaking about the mother or father "within us" and not about the mother or father who is "living in upstate New York." Through clarification of this distinction between parental complexes and actual parents, we can often open an avenue to greater clarification of the immediate distinctions, woman or man versus hag or hero.

Meaning reconstruction in couple therapy, then, is focused especially on differentiating the archetypal complexes of mother, father and animus or anima from personal reality. Emphasizing the difference between emotional states or unconscious motivations, which are compelling and demanding, and personal reality, which is intentional and responsible, should free the partners to use both. Validating both as making sense undermines the heroic position that everything can be solved rationally and that everyone should seek greater control of their emotions. At the same time, it undermines the hag's reality that emotions are always overwhelming and compelling and that nothing can be done about them.

New Learning

The strategy of new learning is implicit in all forms of therapy, even in the social ritual of therapy itself. Because therapy is a unique interpersonal context, we all learn new ways of being by participating in it. Simply responding to the cues that the therapist gives the client engenders new learning: the therapist says, "Come and talk with me intimately, but behave also as though this is a business arrangement by arriving on time, leaving on time and paying me." Behaving impersonally while talking personally involves new learning. Learning the special language of therapy—and all therapies have some special language—is an experience of new learning for most clients.

The conscious strategy of new learning from the therapist's perspective, however, entails the careful planning of tasks that will increase clients' skills and modes of coping with the personal and interpersonal contexts of their lives. In couple therapy, we use at least three techniques to enact our strategy for new learning. These techniques include *homework, videotaping,* and the *therapist interview.*

Homework: Usually tasks are assigned at the conclusion of a session, but they may be given at any point.

An effective homework task should be entirely congruent with the client's conscious desire to change some aspect of her or his life. Do not assign tasks which are confusing or contradictory to conscious understanding. This is a non-paradoxical approach to homework, although the assignment may have a "hidden paradox."

We often assign the task of scheduling intimate time together. On the surface, the partners have asked to be more intimate and the task is congruent with what they want. To "assign time" is somewhat paradoxical, however, and we are asking them to do what they often want to retreat from—more scheduling. If they are ready, this will provoke them to find time on their own, without assigning it. If not, they will schedule the time just to be "good clients," though sometimes resenting our "parental" influence. Whichever way the assignment turns out, it will benefit the therapy.

The homework task of scheduling intimate time is difficult for most couples in middle life, and perhaps for most couples in general. We explain that relationship needs tending in order to survive. Humorously, we sketch a picture of modern life which depicts the contradictory dictates of "romance" and "marriage": most of us spend a great deal of effort in finding the right partner for the intimate life of sharing and comfort we initially envision marriage to be, yet after we find this person we set up a household that requires us to separate from the person for the greater part of every day. It is as though we find a partner in order to lose contact with her or him.

The assignment of intimate time usually has a corollary of "spending it in a leisurely and sexy way." For some couples, this will appropriately involve being assigned time in bed during waking hours so that they restore their physical contact. For others, it will involve doing new things together. We stress the importance of feeling "sexy" and "powerful" in oneself during these times. Dressing up, having sex in unusual places and feeling one's attractiveness are all ideas that are connected with this assignment.

Other homework assignments vary, depending on the stage of therapy and the presenting problem. Concerns involving parenting, developing individual interests, limiting work involvement and carrying out household tasks are all part of our repertoire. In particular, we stress the skills and competence developed through care-giving and the necessity of learning about the tasks that one is drawn to.

In general, homework assignments should be stated in behavioral terms, as clearly as possible. For example, do not say, "Work on the communication difficulties we uncovered in the session." Instead, say, "Each time Louise slams the door to her bedroom, Larry should say to himself, 'She's hurt and she is inviting me into the bedroom,' and then act on the invitation if he so desires."

The therapists' imaginations play a great part in assigning the homework task. Go with your intuition. Something colorful or vivid which crosses your mind during the session is generally better than something you dutifully think up at the end. Consultation between co-therapists is usually required before homework is assigned so that each co-therapist can talk about the images that came up during the session.

Related to homework assignments is the new learning clients gain by seeing themselves in context during therapy. Providing opportunities for the partners to view their interactional field in its archetypal and personal dimensions is a reliable technique for new learning. Videotaping short segments of a therapy session and then reviewing these with the clients is especially useful in this regard.

Videotaping: Videotape all or part of a session with the couple. Select ten minutes which illustrate some essential aspect of a complex or a projection of the anima or animus. Prepare to explore the tape with the couple by watching the segment in advance.

Before viewing the tape in the session, prepare the clients by telling them that they may feel uneasy at first at seeing themselves on videotape. (Being able to see one's whole body in motion is sometimes anxiety-provoking.) Tell the clients to recall their thoughts and feelings from the session as they see themselves on tape. Encourage them to say "stop" when they see or hear something they would like to talk about.

While watching the tape, stop when you can offer insight into a symbolic meaning, a gesture or some other aspect of the interpersonal field which has been unconscious but is meaningful in terms of your work with the couple. Significant gestures can be translated into images or words, and unattended feelings can then be opened up. Each time the tape is stopped, ask each partner what she or he was thinking or feeling at that moment in the session—or what she or he was trying to communicate. Amplify symbolic meanings with images from myth and story, whenever appropriate, to help the couple understand the non-rational dimension of their expressions.

At the end, review any overall themes which emerge in the tape. For example, you may say, "Louise, each time you spoke to Larry, you looked away. I got the impression that you were afraid throughout the whole ten minutes. What about this?"

We have videotaped ourselves in a few of these recall sessions with couples and have found this useful for our own learning too. It has allowed us to review our ability to analyze the interpersonal field "at a distance."

Using videotape fits well with teaching new personal modes of communication. Examples of non-empathic responding and projecting one's own thoughts and feelings can be used to contrast with empathic responding. We often teach client couples to use the communication skills which are taught to beginning counseling students. For example, we teach each person to speak directly from her or his experience rather than attribute feelings to the other. Attributing one's own discomfort to another is stated in terms like, "You're mad at me." A more empathic personal statement would be, "I feel uncomfortable and wonder if you are mad at me."

Another communication skill which commonly helps people separate themselves from complexes is responding to angry and aggressive attacks with a statement which reflects what the attack has meant or felt like, instead of responding defensively. When Larry shouts at Louise, saying, "You're just bitchy today and nothing I say makes any difference," Louise can respond by saying, "In other words, I haven't responded to *anything* you've said. I get very angry when you make such extreme statements." By reflecting Larry's words and staying with her own experience, Louise avoids projecting her personal agency onto Larry by saying something like, "You *make me* so mad."

In general, we teach people to avoid saying that others *make* them feel or believe anything. Such externalization of responsibility creates confusion between a complex and a person. Other people do not make us feel one way or another; rather, we respond to others through our own complexes or assumptions. (For example, an angry stranger shouting obscenities in the street rarely makes the passersby mad. They avoid him or laugh because he does not "hook" anything emotional in them.) We are not at all indifferent to others' emotions; we simply create a context in ourselves for experiencing the stimulation of others.

Learning empathic communication of feelings (differentiating one's own responses from the interpersonal environment) is generally quite useful for clarifying confused communications. Using the videotape in a "recall" process provides a natural vehicle for learning new response modes.

Imitation of the therapist couple is another vehicle for new learning. Therefore we have *therapist interviews* several times throughout each session. Generally we have one near the beginning of the session, after we have had the couple engage in some activity, and then again before the final wrap-up at the end. (This procedure was briefly described as part of the initial assessment.)

Therapist Interview: The co-therapists sit in the clients' chairs or simply face one another, blocking the clients from their field of vision. The therapists assess their observations of communication patterns, complexes, non-rational expressions and individual client functioning. Ordinary descriptive language is used (no special jargon), and examples are given to illustrate what is being described. The therapists use empathic responding and feeling statements and "check out" their own accuracy of observations with each other. They are modeling empathic communication. The therapists may also role-play the client couple.

When the interview is over (usually it lasts 3-5 minutes), the therapists pull their chairs into a circle with the clients and use the same communication modes to talk with the clients about their experience of what they just heard.

This form of "in-session" assessment is informative at both symbolic and rational levels. The content of the therapist interview concerns differentiating the archetypal and the personal. The form of the interview involves showing the clients how they can collaborate even though they may have differences. Typically, we find that this intervention is readily appreciated by clients and brings humor and relief into our session, especially when we role-play the clients.

The basic strategy of new learning in couple therapy, then, concerns the therapists and clients working together to develop new skills, modes of action and perspectives in interpersonal relating.

Expansion of Vocabulary for Meaning Making

This strategy, like new learning, is developed throughout most experiences in therapy. Simply put, the strategy involves expanding the client's vocabulary and use of language so that she or he can develop greater clarity and imagination in verbal expression. Facilitating the use of new words and sentences to explain human motivation, responsibility, personal agency and vivid feelings is the basis of this method.

Techniques like *interpretation* and *reframing* are normally means for expanding the vocabulary of personal meaning of clients in therapy. Interpretation involves assigning a new meaning to an old experience, or penetrating an old meaning with a new one. Reframing is the technique of giving a different meaning context for an event reported by a client—e.g., talking about a child's acting out in the classroom as her caring expression of the family's hurt. Interpretation and reframing bring insight or understanding of an experience or state of being that was previously inaccessible to the client. When a client learns how to interpret her or his own experiences, then no experience has only one meaning; rather, different ways of describing and finding meaning are created. A person is thereby "freed" to understand an event from both personal and archetypal points of view.

Two techniques we use with couples contribute to increasing vocabulary for meaning making and allow partners to get a new perspective on events. They are *role reversal*, a technique which derives from psychodrama, and *trading places*, a variation on role reversal.

Role Reversal: Members of the couple are directed to exchange roles with each other in discussing a charged topic. Each partner is instructed to "look like, feel like and talk like" the other. Time is taken for each person to arrange posture and clothing so as to experience the other's perspective as fully as possible. They are told to use the other person's language.

Partners carry out a ten to fifteen minute interview in these reversed roles. The co-therapists may double the partners during the role reversal interview. After the interview is finished, the co-therapists pull their chairs into a circle with the clients and talk about the experience.

In recalling the thoughts and feelings experienced in the other role, clients should be helped to emphasize the difference in perspective or framework that was engendered by using the other's language and posture.

Role reversal interviews can also be enacted by the therapists, who then play each other.

Exchange of perspectives permits insight into the non-rational levels of expression and into the influence of language on emotional responses. Additionally, the co-therapists have a good opportunity to assess how closely each partner has observed and understood the other. We have discovered that the woman is often a good mimic of the man, but that the reverse is rarely true. Knowing that one partner has a gap in her or his ability to observe and understand the other accurately is important information.

In the later stages of therapy, we sometimes engage in *trading places.* In this technique, the client couple becomes the therapist couple while the therapists become the clients. This exercise is enacted as a role-play, with the clients imitating the therapists and the therapists imitating the clients.

Trading Places: The co-therapists move into the clients' chairs and assume the typical postures of the clients. Each therapist plays the same-sexed client. The clients move into the therapists' chairs and assume their typical postures. The co-therapists discuss a charged topic as though they were the client couple, using typical gestures and language of each client. The clients attempt to double the therapists or to ask questions and make interpretations. The clients are instructed to behave just as they have seen the therapists behave.

Usually this kind of interview lasts barely five minutes because of the anxiety it creates in the client couple, who are forced to see many different sides of their interpersonal field. When the clients seem ready to "give in," the interview should be stopped and chairs placed in a circle so that everyone can discuss what happened. Clients are usually stimulated to many new levels of meaning in this interchange of roles.

A simpler format is to have the therapists role-play the client couple while the clients watch.

Much material related to complexes and to personal awareness is generated both in role reversal and in trading places. Shifting perspective on the world of meaning provides an avenue for greater understanding of all three realities: archetype as such (gestural), archetypal-complex (implied symbolic) and personal (narrative).

Expanding the perspective and vocabulary for meaning making often results in a new "relativism" in one's point of view on the interpersonal field. People are less likely to blame the other person for their own dissatisfactions after taking the other's point of view. When these techniques work to expand meaning, clients emerge with a greater appreciation of how language, posture and gesture affect meaning for individuals.

Sometimes this intervention does not work well and is confusing to the clients. If clients seem confused or too anxious in hearing these activities explained, it is best for co-therapists to demonstrate them first. After the demonstration there should be a readiness or sense of ease in the clients. If this is absent, then it is probably best for only the co-therapists to use the techniques. Role reversal and role-playing are difficult activities that require a high level of integration and empathic responding. When people are in crisis, or especially anxious, naturally these techniques are contraindicated.

Expansion of attitudes and vocabulary for new meaning is a strategy which works directly on the current conscious attitude of the client. Through activities involving new perspectives, clients are encouraged to change their frameworks or paradigms for making meaning out of experience.

Format of Sessions

In order to clarify even further exactly what we do, I will briefly review the typical structure of a two-hour session with a couple. Of course, no structure is really "typical" because we ad-lib in every session and often encounter material we had not anticipated. Still, we have a rule of thumb.

In the first ten to fifteen minutes, we usually have the couple interact while we watch. Partly we are "warming up" while "charging" them up a bit with the anxiety of being on stage. Either they will talk about a current concern, or they will talk about their homework. Sometimes, if we have noticed a theme in our wrap-up from the previous session, we will direct them to talk about something which did not get adequate attention—e.g., "Talk about your sex life lately."

Usually we have a brief therapist interview next and then go into doubling or to an empathy interview. If emotions are intense, especially anger or hurt, we find that the empathy interview is the best way to work. In the interview, the focus on only one client and the observation of the two other people function to "contain" some of the emotional charge. At the beginning of a session in which strong feelings are expressed, containment is the best first step. Acting out of complexes can be quite destructive in a couple session if the therapists are not able to manage the event. Aggression and hostility can rupture basic trust in the session just as they can in the couple relationship.

After our first intervention and discussion of it with the clients, we often take a brief break in order to plan the rest of the session. We will choose some theme or topic which has come up in the first part of the session and see how it fits into the general understanding we have of the negative mother complex from the Gawain-Ragnell story. We may allow the story to lead us to our next intervention. If the hag needs to give her answer, then we work with the woman to give her a voice. If the hero is collecting facts and data, we may deal in facts and data to back our point or we may work with the hag to confront him. Specific images from the story—e.g., the hero "losing his head" and the hag "living out in the woods"—recur in all our discussions about the couple. We do not take the story as a literal guide for how to conduct therapy; rather, we use it as a backdrop for our own imaginations. Phrases like "out in the woods" or "sovereignty, the right to rule your own life" have become dear to us and we often use them verbatim in our sessions. Themes from the story, such as the importance of property to men's well-being and of physical appearance to women's well-being, are always present as reminders in everything we plan and do. Our discussion breaks during sessions provide us with opportunities to listen to the story and think out our plans.

We prefer that the last approximately forty minutes of the session be quite intense emotionally. Therefore, we will deal with the "hottest" topic during this time. Our reasoning for this is that the couple will leave with a high motivation to go on working when they are emotionally aroused. Moreover, they will discover that together they can comfort and contain the emotions which are agitated in therapy. In choosing a hot topic for our concluding interventions, we pick the issue that the couple seems to be hiding or refusing to talk about. This may be the problem of an outside lover, financial debt, step-children or any number of other common issues of difference among couples. In part, we want to show them the way to bring their secrets out into language and thereby increase the experience of trust between them. The techniques we most often use during the last forty minutes include doubling, role reversal and some kind of role playing. These interventions arouse feelings and involve activity and drama.

We leave at least ten minutes (fifteen is better) for closing the session. Seated in a circle with the couple, we ask both partners what they have learned individually in the session. We talk about what we have learned and assign homework based on the learning. In summarizing our observations, we find it especially useful to talk in terms of "You are the type of people who . . . " or "You are the type of person who . . . " In this way, we elicit concern for identity in each person. In a manner of speaking, this formulation allows us to confront the current conscious attitude in each personality.

Finally, we are active in our sessions. Rarely do the therapists remain seated in the same chairs for more than ten minutes. We shift around in our doubling and use of different interview formats in what might appear to be a "dance between therapists." The physical movements to take different roles or imply different meanings lend excitement to the sessions. Whenever possible, we introduce humor to increase both our ability and the clients' ability to get some new perspective on what is happening.

Stages of Couple Therapy

Returning to each of the stages reviewed in the last chapter, I will state briefly the kinds of interventions we use most often and our usual underlying strategies.

The Desire to Dominate

Most couples enter therapy at this stage, in the midst of dominance-submission problems. Our major task initially is, of course, to assess their ability and willingness to stay together. If basic trust seems to have been completely lost, and one or both partners has indicated a strong desire to separate, then we work toward separation in one or two sessions. Separation plans involve mediation of differences in order to settle property and custody agreements. We use empathy interviews and some doubling in working toward separation agreements. If both people are interested in continuing their relationship, then we work with them confrontatively in the first two sessions.

Confrontation with loss, listening to the partner's reality and confrontation with one's own complexes are the themes in the first two

interviews at this stage. We most often use the techniques of doubling, therapist interviews and empathy interviews. Our underlying
strategy is to manage the rapport of the couple relationship in order
to prod each individual toward a recognition of the need to change.
Feelings of hopelessness and despairing frustration sometimes provoke such intense emotions that we separately interview each of the
partners in different rooms. Each therapist spends about ten minutes
with the same-sexed partner of the client couple in attempting to
establish a clear understanding of that client's needs and fears regarding some aspect of the relationship. Separate interviews are also
conducted during one of the first two sessions in order to take a
sexual history of each partner (see appendix for the framework for
psychosexual assessment).

Our goals in this phase, as we described them in the last chapter,
are to motivate each partner to confront the hag within and to open
up communication channels for the development of objective empathy between them. We may use some listening skills in teaching the
partners how to speak and respond more openly during this phase.

What Do Women Really Want?

Some couples enter therapy at this stage. The "liberated" or
"feminist" couple will present themselves as Ragnell and Gawain at
the wedding banquet. She is the hag who prods and provokes emotional scenes, and she feels a certain authority in doing so. She
"knows" that emotional contact and true sharing of ordinary life are
essential concerns for their relationship. Yet she appears bitter, depressed or angry both about her insights and about the feeling of
deadness in the couple relationship. The man is patient, seemingly
responsive to his wife's needs and ideas, and extremely rational. He
is the willing but stupid hero. Together they "just don't know what is
wrong" because they seem to have tried all of the collective solutions
to their problems, such as "dividing up the chores" around the
house and his "giving her freedom" to develop herself in the ways
she has demanded.

Our task with partners at this stage is to increase their empathy
for one another and convince them both of the value of the feminine
in their lives. Of course, the task entails withdrawing the projections
of hag and hero. The idea of sovereignty, in terms of allowing each
person to develop her or his own way of enacting the feminine,
while continuing to individuate, is the guiding idea. Our strategies
include managing the rapport, meaning reconstruction and new
learning. We use the techniques of empathy interviews, doubling,

videotaping and role playing to assist us. We try to keep our focus on the secret or hidden issues implied by the couple. These will involve the marital contract which was broken earlier and the results of injured basic trust between them.

Increasing intimacy between the partners, stimulating their sexual feelings and desire for contact, and removing barriers to basic trust are our goals. Usually we cannot accomplish these straightforwardly because the resistance is great. In withdrawing projections, through learning about non-rational expression and "hearing the complexes speak," each person is confronted with old wishes and impulses.

On the man's part, these generally involve his fear of being overwhelmed and dominated by a negative mother. When his projections of the hag are withdrawn, he discovers that his own moods and fears have been destructive, not only toward his family but toward others as well. He feels guilty and angry about lost possibilities for relationship and involvement with others. He may temporarily remove himself by withdrawing into depression, or he may retreat to the bully posture of anger and temper tantrums. Either way, he must be convinced, again and again, through both experience and rational explanation, that his regression will lead nowhere. The "nowhere" is interpreted generally as loss, death and stagnation.

For the woman, her fears involve abandonment. She will be terrified of her own inner bully, who dominates and deserts her. She will have great difficulty with the idea that her development is her business; it is her own choice, and depends on her agency. The idea of submission (not subservience) is prominent for her as she must learn to submit to her own creative urges and to the tenderness and nurturance of her partner. That she should *trust* him to provide both sexual and household care will come as a surprise. She *wishes* he would provide care her way and her way only, and she fears that she is really "not good enough" to be tenderly supported. She may withdraw through self-hatred into a confused and fragmented self. Rather than take on the tasks of becoming a vital and enthusiastic woman (sometimes called "sexy" or "beautiful" by us), she will complain about her lack of resources (her body is fat, wrinkled, old, unavailable; she is not properly educated, articulate, etc.). She must be reinforced in her strength, as a mother and as a knowing woman. She must also be confronted with the loss and depression which she must face if she refuses this task.

At this stage, we focus a good deal of our conceptualization on practical feminist concerns. The oppression of women, ignorance about their sexual and emotional life, lack of reinforcement for care-

giving activities and lack of opportunities for female heroism are topics we often take up in doubling or empathy interviews.

Empathy, Authority and Trust

When we have reached this stage, both people are once again
"themselves." Each one has acquired an authentic, individual voice
and ideas for re-establishing intimacy and trust. We allow them to
lead us toward their final resolution, in terms of how they want to
rearrange their actual homelife and worklife in order to incorporate a
new intimacy in their relationship. We expect to see evidence of both
empathy and authority within the couple relationship, in and out of
sessions.

We use all of the strategies we have described at this point, but
we emphasize new learning and increasing the vocabulary for meaning making. The partners will be taking their therapy with them into
their ordinary daily lives, and they need to know how to seek further
resources as well as how to continue to use the ones we have
provided. They can benefit from reading, listening to taped material
and going to lectures which concern individuation through couple
relationship. They can also benefit from videotaping, role reversal
and role playing within the sessions. The focus is on internalizing
what has been learned in the therapy so that the couple can continue to do therapy themselves within their own relationship. Using
dream interpretation, suggesting individual therapy for one or both
(when appropriate) and surveying community resources for support
networks (involving childcare, contact with similar couples, etc.) are
means for helping the partners internalize their therapy.

The final session should ideally have an element of celebration in
it. This does not mean giving a party for the couple, although a
party atmosphere is appropriate when it is authentic. Rather, it
means that the therapist couple provides a means for "joining" with
the client couple to establish a feeling of mutual learning and reciprocity based on trust between the two couples. We generally talk
about what we have learned from the client couple and how they
have enriched our lives. We send them off with good wishes and
remind them that we will meet for a follow-up in six months.

Follow-Up

If the therapy has worked well, the follow-up session should be a
little dull. We conduct it like an initial assessment and have the
couple begin by talking to each other about what they hope to get
from the therapy session. If they have internalized the work of

therapy, we will hear them say something like, "Well, we are here because we had to come, but really nothing is wrong between us that we cannot fix ourselves." Like the family doctor, my co-therapist and I "poke around" at the complex a bit and see if we can activate anything that seems hidden. If we cannot, we say so immediately and give them a "clean bill of health." The remainder of the session can then be used in whatever way the couple directs.

If the partners have retreated to some earlier phase in their work, then we take up therapy at that stage. We plan additional sessions, depending on what we see, in order to repair what has been injured in the six-month period. We listen closely to what the clients tell us about "why therapy hasn't worked," to assess how our own failures as therapists may have contributed. Did our complexes interfere with the therapy? Did we fail to pay enough attention to their environmental stresses, to someone's resistance, to someone's vulner- abilities? This is a point for serious self-examination on the part of the therapists. After the therapists have consulted between them- selves about the assessment, the results should be reported directly to the client couple, including what the therapists see as their own failures or responsibility for what was lost.

We strive to confine our work with couples to six sessions with a six-month follow-up. This is a good container for our own wishes and fears. We believe that co-therapists (ourselves very much in- cluded) tend to "live out" aspects of the client couple. Without a limitation to their contact with the couple, the co-therapists risk becoming the client couple through their efforts to "cure" or out of their jealousy of the couple's financial, intellectual or other re- sources. Containing the therapy helps to restrain the therapist couple from becoming too involved with the client couple. Conceptualizing the couple relationship as the *frame* for therapy also helps to empha- size that the essential work is done within that relationship and not between the two couples.

Therapist Training

Ongoing education through workshops and reading is essential for doing couple therapy; one can never learn enough. We attend fam- ily therapy demonstrations, read the literature on relationship ther- apy and strive to develop our own model of integrating symbolic interpretation into active therapy with couples. Our own background includes many orientations to psychotherapy. Those we consider essential for doing adequate couple therapy are behavioral, psychodynamic (especially Jungian), cognitive and some form of active group or family intervention—such as psychodrama, structural family therapy or strategic family therapy. Without at least this much range in one's ability to use techniques, therapists can easily become blocked or overwhelmed by their couple clients. The technique of interpretation is probably the one we use most often, but it is usually accompanied by something more active such as doubling or role playing. Naturally, one's own therapy, especially relationship therapy, is also essential for doing this kind of work.

Working with couples has become the "leading edge" in our practice of psychotherapy. My co-therapist and I feel that we have been educated and expanded by our experiences with people struggling like ourselves to maintain the vitality of human contact at the center of their lives.

7

Identification with a Complex versus Enactment

In order to make decisions about strategy and technique in doing psychotherapy, we must first concern ourselves with the *person* of the client. Although the presenting problem is certainly a matter for serious consideration, that problem cannot be adequately understood until we know something about the personal reality of the client. What frame of reference does the client bring to the treatment situation, and how available is this person to the influence of the therapist's particular methods and style?

The process of assessing a person for treatment in psychotherapy is complex and multilayered. Our initial assessment for couple therapy attends to the developmental functioning of the members of the couple and their readiness for the insight-oriented, self-reflective techniques that we use. (In the appendix, I offer an outline for making a complete developmental and contextual assessment.) In this chapter, we will look at only one aspect: the distinction between *identification* with an unconscious complex and an occasional *enactment* of unconscious complexes in an habitual way.

In order to clarify this important distinction, let us review the early process of individuation. Personal identity (Jung's "ego complex") emerges gradually through the de-integration and re-integration of psychological complexes. The experienced unity of self-other, depicted imagistically as a circle or as the Great Round in creation mythologies, initially de-integrates or breaks up into affective schemata organized around archetypal images. I have referred to these as archetypal complexes to indicate that they are unconscious and infused with emotional-instinctual energy. The ordinary complexes of everyday life in the first part of the lifespan are mother, father, god (or world), and self and not-self. The complex organized around the experience of subjectivity, body-being and agency is archetypal in terms of the standard organization of the human personality toward coherence and continuity, but it becomes personal as the identity complex is referred to the experience of being a person-among-persons. This experience of being a person has several hallmarks which set it apart from being an animal or a divinity: self-reflection, personal responsibility, acknowledged recognition of one's ability to anticipate consequences and direct one's own behavior, and knowledge of the finitude of the individual lifespan. The achievement of these features of personal identity occurs gradually, usually during the period from about nine months until about eighteen or nineteen years of age. Other characteristics of personal identity (such as attributions about gender) are also important to the understanding of personality, but the features listed here are sufficient for our discussion.

As an individual differentiates a personal identity, she or he integrates the mother and father complexes into personal awareness, both in terms of becoming a potential mother or father and in terms of distinguishing between the archetypal complexes and the people who reared one as a child. Withdrawing and integrating psychological complexes projected onto mother, father, sister and brother form one arena for achieving a personal identity in adulthood.

Until the mother and father complexes are at least partly integrated into personal identity, the individual is not able to function as a responsible and self-reflective person. Instead, she or he is prone to being overwhelmed by unconscious complexes and acting out the archetypal meanings of the complexes. The hag and bully roles of the negative mother complex are enactments of the habitual, emotionally charged schemata of the Terrible Mother archetype. The hag identifies herself with the Terrible Mother and the bully reacts to her as though she were the dragon who must be fought and killed.

When these archetypal roles are repeatedly enacted within the interpersonal field of the couple, they become habitual and exciting, and come to replace the sexual excitement and shared interests of the couple. If the problem in the couple relationship is indeed within the interpersonal field of their relationship, the individuals will be free to act otherwise when they are apart or engaged interpersonally with someone other than the partner. If the couple's problem includes developmental difficulties on the part of one or both partners, however, there will be no evidence of this kind of freedom from the complex. When either one or both members is wholly identified with the hag or bully, and does not have a personal identity, the individual(s) will appear consistently to have the same communication difficulties that are evidenced in the couple relationship. Rather than confining the enactments of fear and rage to the couple relationship, the individual(s) will act these out in a number of different settings and with different persons.

Our method of assessment in the initial interview allows us to speak empathically with each individual separately, if we choose. During the empathy interview, the therapist will be able to assess the capacity of the individual to be free of the complex and to respond personally—that is, self-reflectively and responsibly—to the concerns of treatment.

On Being and Doing the Hag

When a woman is wholly identified with the hag role in the negative mother complex, she is functioning at the first stage of animus development. Her response to men and males is one of basic distrust; she is not able to reflect on herself in a sustained, objective way; and she will quickly become de-integrated when she is anxious. When in a state of de-integration, she will respond out of different and sometimes conflicting unconscious complexes and will appear not to be concerned about the discontinuity of her behavior. For example, the woman may say she wants her husband to help out more around the house; yet when questioned about it, she might state that she wants him to "keep his nose out of my business." Although the hag-enacting woman, who is at a later stage of development, can also speak in such a discontinuous way, she will acknowledge the incongruities when interviewed by the therapist. When the hag-identified woman is questioned by the therapist, she may offer a weak rationalization for the incongruity, or she may not see any discontinuity in her contrasting statements.

Of primary concern for our form of treatment, the hag-identified woman will not be able to distinguish between metaphorical and literal reality. A common distinction that such a woman will find impossible is, for example, the distinction between hearing and listening. When asked whether or not her husband listened to something she said, she will say something like, "Oh yes, he *heard* me." When this distinction is explored with her, she will not be able to acknowledge any difference between being heard and being understood. Metaphorical expressions of feeling states will escape her attention or confuse her; in fact, she can become extremely frustrated, anxious and de-integrated if the therapist speaks in metaphorical terms when she is speaking in literal and concrete ones.

In her own development, such a hag-identified woman has not achieved "emotional object constancy" or the consistently reliable ability to distinguish her own thoughts and feelings from those of another, especially a significant other. Most often she is "fused" with her mother or her sisters and reports that her values and behaviors are exactly consistent with theirs. She experiences her thoughts and feelings in somewhat undifferentiated ways: her feelings "upset" her and her thoughts "happen" to her. She functions daily with a lot of wishing and fearing, through wish fulfillment and passive dependency. Although she may act out her aggressive feelings, she will deny their meaning and see her actions as only reactive or "controlled" by another. For example, she may beat her children because "they make me mad."

Evidence of her typical defenses against the de-integration of anxiety will emerge even in the first interview, which can be quite anxiety-provoking. The therapist will see many instances of "splitting," of good-bad, right-wrong, nice-mean evaluations. Similarly, the therapist will experience this woman's "projective identification" as the woman attributes her own feelings to another—often the therapist—and then reacts against them. Concrete idealization and imitation of authority figures, usually female ones, will be evident, as they will have replaced personal decision making and responsibility in this woman's actions. She may carry out complex actions simply because her mother does them and her mother is "a good woman." Her denial of feelings, and even of the physical reality around her, will be obvious. Denial functions to eliminate large areas of awareness, whereas repression (a more differentiated defense) is selective in its elimination of only certain threatening aspects of interpersonal reality. A woman who is fairly consistently identified with *being* the Great or Terrible Mother does not show a repertoire of personal responses even when she is outside of the interpersonal field of the couple relationship.

The woman who is temporarily and conflictually *doing* the hag role will identify with it only in the interpersonal field in which it is habitually enacted. She will not consistently carry this identity elsewhere. Therefore, when she is speaking with the therapist, she can function self-reflectively and responsibly even in relation to her hag-identified enactments in the complex. In speaking with the therapist, she will appear more flexible, more able to translate between metaphorical and literal reality, and more objective about her own behavior. Usually she will indicate her own desire to disidentify with the hag and to be free of the habitual enactments of the complex with her partner. The hag role will seem "ego dystonic" to her because it is not a part of her personal identity.

On Being and Doing the Bully

The bully role is depicted consistently in terms of certain assumptions and behaviors. As an identity state, the bully is a defensive posture involving aggressive and dominance behaviors *against* a force (usually a "feminine" force) which seems chaotically overwhelming. The bully reacts against the Terrible Mother, who is at once his own unconscious feeling life *and* the power of the female other—the original mother. Physical and emotional abuse are enacted due to the threat of the Terrible Mother who will dominate and de-integrate the bully if he does not fight her.

As an enduring identity state, the bully role will compel a man into aggressive and impulsive fighting behavior in many different situations. He will not be able to distinguish between authority and aggression, between loving concern and dominance, and between feelings and actions. The man who has habituated in the bully identity is ridden by his impulses and by fears of his impulses. Because most of the impulses are aggressive and destructive, they get him into trouble. He cannot figure out why he is often singled out as troublesome because he cannot anticipate the consequences of his own actions and believes that his actions are always justified. This kind of man learns only through environmental rewards and punishments; he is not motivated either by approval or by love. Because he cannot trust others—especially female others—he must constantly defend against his feelings of tenderness and love. Rather than experience feelings of tenderness, he feels driven by needs and urges that must be gratified if he is to function at all. Because these needs seem to be insatiable, he may talk about constant frustration and even fear of his own feelings.

Like the woman who has adapted at the stage of animus as Alien Other, the bully-identified man has an impoverished vocabulary for articulating an inner life. He is "okay," "pissed," or "upset" rather than angry, fearful, content or joyful. Also similar to the hag-identified woman, he uses the defenses of splitting, projective identification and denial more often than other defenses against anxiety. Because he may be reinforced for his macho image and behavior by a culture which values male aggression, he may find his violent acting out of reactions against dominance to be socially rewarded. In such rewarding contexts he can become quite physically dangerous without feeling any shame or fear about his behavior.

In therapy sessions, the bully-identified man is potentially dangerous if he is provoked into de-integration. The therapists can assess, through an empathy interview, such a man's personal responses to his bully enactments. Whenever physical and sexual abuse of partner or children has been reported, such assessment is essential. Even when bully enactments are contained within the couple relationship, if the man is provoked by the therapists he may become dangerous to his partner during the course of therapy. The degree to which violent and abusive behaviors are "dystonic" to the man should be a guiding feature in the therapist's decision concerning his readiness for our form of couple therapy.

In general, we have found that a man who has repeatedly enacted violent abuse without consequence outside of the couple relationship needs to be told directly to "stop." If the man has a personal identity, he will ally himself immediately with this therapeutic guidance. If he is identified with the bully, however, he will retreat and seem to "hide" from the therapist's injunction. Our form of therapy is contraindicated if the man does not agree to stop acting out his aggressive impulses.

The man who is temporarily and conflictually *doing* the bully role within the couple relationship will necessarily experience an anxious drop in his self-esteem when he is confronted by the therapists concerning the destructiveness of his behavior. At the time of initial confrontation, he should be supported, without excessive admonition, in the direction of change. If he appears to be self-reflective, to enact his bullying only within the couple relationship, and to desire responsible control of his behavior, he is acceptable for doing the kind of work we have described.

The other side of impulsive acting out in the bully role is impulsive "acting in," or aggression turned against the self. This kind of behavior usually involves drugs, alcohol or suicidal threats. These impulsive behaviors must also be assessed initially and monitored throughout treatment.

The bully-identified man who has not developed a secure personal identity should be treated individually and immediately referred out of the couple therapy procedure. The bully-enacting man can be treated within our format, but he is vulnerable to his impulses much more than is the hero-identified man who may occasionally enact the bully.

Alternative Forms of Treatment

When one or both partners have not differentiated a personal identity, they can be referred to other forms of treatment, either to accompany or replace the couple therapy. Usually we treat the hag-identified woman or bully-identified man individually. If both individuals have fairly primitive defenses and are easily de-integrated by anxiety, then we do not proceed with couple therapy at all. If only one person has developmental difficulties, he or she can be treated individually while both participate in a course of couple therapy. Many factors, such as financial and other life circumstances, will enter into the final decision to be made if the members of a couple are not both ready to begin treatment together.

When an individual has habituated through identifying with a parental complex, or reacting against it, then a number of treatment approaches can be used to further development of personal identity. Most of these are "psychoeducational" or "manipulative" rather than "insight-oriented." The director of therapy is the therapist and a wholly collaborative symbolic field is not engaged openly in the therapy. The therapist may monitor and assess the symbolic field, but will not communicate this verbally to the client.

The bully-identified man is most likely to change through environmental rewards and punishments. Therefore, behavioral methods of intervention (manipulations by the therapist rather than a self-control program) are most effective. The appropriate tasks of therapy include increasing verbal skills in describing events and actions in a personal mode. This would involve teaching and rewarding language which is used to identify feeling states, rather than the direct acting out or "acting in" of impulses. Social skills and delayed gratification can often be taught more effectively in structured group therapy than in individual therapy. Parent effectiveness training has been helpful, for example, in teaching abusive men how to parent their children without responding aggressively to misbehaviors. Self-management skills, such as housekeeping and cooking, can also be taught and rewarded. Perhaps most important is the teaching of personal trust by giving the client opportunities to speak and listen to others in a protected environment, usually in a group.

Similar forms of treatment can be used with the hag-identified woman, but she can be exposed to some other methods as well. Because she does not usually have the problem of troublesome, impulsive acting out (although she may), she can be available to more sophisticated interventions such as Reality Therapy, in which rational modes are taught and consequences of behavior are mapped out. She can learn how to seek her own rewards and avoid punishment by anticipating interpersonal responses from others. The therapist can reward her conforming behaviors, which indicate trust, through approval. She can be taught to trust through interpersonal rewards, rather than material rewards. (The bully-habituated man may respond better to concrete or material rewards.) Usually this kind of woman can learn the difference between long and short-term goals and can set behavioral goals for herself as she learns how to develop greater independence. Identifying with peers rather than authority figures should be encouraged, and the woman should be supported for forming friendships, especially for developing a relationship of trust with a "chum" outside of her family of origin.

Individuals who are treated through these more supportive and educational forms of therapy may be able to return for couple therapy at some point. A modified form of couple therapy is preferable to the more metaphorical and imaginative form we have described. Agreeing on specific goals for behavioral change and helping the hag and bully to become more equal partners in parenting or other sharing will encourage the individuals to see each other as persons. As the clients change, through therapeutic help, they should be re-assessed for their potential to function primarily with a personal identity. Occasionally we have worked with middle-aged people who seemed "prone to develop" and responded quite quickly to individual treatment of the kind I have described. Usually, however, when people have identified with the hag and bully roles of the negative mother complex for a substantial period of their adult lives, they need time and patience in order to recognize and integrate these roles into a personal identity.

Much more is involved in developmental assessment than I have sketched out in this chapter. In order to assess cognitive, interpersonal and moral functioning in an individual, the therapist has to examine a variety of activities, thoughts and behaviors (including dreams) in a person's life context.

By and large, individuals are suited to our type of couple therapy if they are not wholly identified with the hag or bully role. Temporary enactments of these roles occur at all stages of development, even in the most individuated and integrated people. By distinguishing an enduring identity from a temporary enactment, the therapist has assessed only one area of interpersonal functioning, the client's response to the archetypal mother complex. From our experience, this singular assessment is sufficient for making a judgment as to the client's suitability for couple therapy. Clearly, in other forms of treatment and even in this form, the therapist may want to assess other areas of functioning in order to make decisions about strategy and technique.

end

8

Conclusion: Vitality through Connection

> *We exist now in a time of doubt about modes of*
> *continuity and connection. . . . Awareness of our*
> *historical predicament—of threats posed by nuclear*
> *weapons, environmental destruction, and the press of*
> *rising population against limited resources—has created*
> *extensive imagery of extinction. These threats occur at a*
> *time when . . . psychohistorical dislocation has already*
> *undermined established symbols around the institutions*
> *of family, church, government, and education.*[1]

We are confronted daily with images of dissolution and disintegration, not only by our news media but also in the neighborhood and among family members. Threats to stability, continuity and integrity emerge from such societal influences as massive weaponry and from such personal experiences as gender identity. Very little of our interpersonal or personal existence seems to be reliably connected to tradition, to a predictable future or even to a solid symbolic context of human meaning. The development of the individual through the life cycle often appears to be unpredictable in the extreme, impinged upon by social and historical upheavals that are unforeseen and unforeseeable.

A couple struggling to re-establish basic trust, a sense of vitality and continuity of being, is faced with obstacles in self and society that often seem insurmountable. The members of the couple bear a daily burden of alienation, resentment, hurt and despair within a social context that provides few guidelines for developing a "rebirth" of meaning from the pain of broken trust. Seeing other couples breaking up, obvious conflicts and unhappiness in long-standing couples, and the "younger generation's" apparent obliviousness to the serious social issues facing them are just some of the stresses that exacerbate despair.

The inspiration that we have felt in our couples work with the Gawain and Ragnell story has run counter to the collective trend toward disintegration. Time and again we have been amazed by the emotional resources couples brought to the work of revitalizing the relationship *after* they could perceive the hope and meaning of doing so. Prior to establishing a context of meaning in which the individuals can clearly see some reasons for changing their behavior,

153

the members of distrusting couples will tend to subvert the recon-
structive work of therapeutic intervention.

Our primary method for entering into a symbolic context is confrontation with loss. We have found that the theme of loss—separation from something or someone with which one has identified
oneself—provides a way into a new meaning system. When people
deny and ignore the potential loss of what is cherished in their
relationship (such as friendship, sexual pleasure, shared parenting
and shared work), they continue to entertain the impossible wishes
of childhood. Confrontation with loss provides a shock to the stagnating and alienating routines of the negative mother complex,
which are played out daily in the hag, hero and bully roles. The
archetypal emotional arousal of these roles will have gradually over-
powered the excitement of a truly shared personal life. Recognition
of loss restores the personal meaning—concerning human empathy,
responsibility and mortality—to the couple's experience.

After the shock of loss has awakened a new desire to embrace the
relationship, the partners must struggle very hard not to lose the
symbolic meaning (the "larger picture") of their life together. In a
social environment which is predicated on individualism, separation,
discontinuity—and even to some extent on real isolation from a
connection to the planet and the universe—the struggle for continuity of trust is indeed heroic.

As I indicated earlier, trust in adult bonding is grounded in
mutuality and equality. Relationship between peers, the archetypal
image of the brother-sister pair, is the model for adult bonding—not
the attachment relationship between parent and child. In Blumstein
and Schwartz's recent massive study of American couples, they discovered that a predominant theme in the reasons why couples survive and the reasons why they break up is women's desire for
equality.[2] In the areas of money, work and sex studied by the
authors, they discovered that women in both lesbian and heterosexual couples valued the ideal of equality over and above many other
features of their relationships. Men in gay relationships assumed
equality with each other much more than did people in other types
of couple relationships.

Women's struggle for equality in partnership is often interpreted
as the "downfall" of marriage, as the basic fault in our current
family system. Contrary to such an interpretation (which is often
based on a dominance-submission model of marriage as a replica of
parent-child bonding), I believe that the current struggle for equality
is the source of new vitality in relationship. As women and men
become more able to shape their relationships through mutuality of

trust and respect, they become able to move more toward a rejuven-
ative bond of *communitas* or shared meaning.

The force of change in marital relationships is perhaps most
apparent in the increasing financial responsibilities carried by
women in the family or couple. With this responsibility comes a new
kind of personal authority and a new kind of sharing. Blumstein and
Schwartz suggest that the institution of marriage has already
changed due to the shift away from the family wage system (and a
single breadwinner) in contemporary society:

> There have already been revisions in the concept of marriage that
> may prove shattering. Society now questions whether husbands should
> have absolute authority. Soon it may be taken for granted that the
> working wife will be a financial partner, sharing even the man's
> provider role. This gives a woman more power because many of the
> justifications for the couple's division of labor were predicated on one
> person, the male, directing the relationship because his work made
> survival possible. If he is no longer the provider, he may lose his
> legitimacy as ultimate decision-maker. . . . Changes such as these do
> not simply modify the institution; they alter the very meaning of
> marriage so drastically that it may cease to be an institution in the
> way we have always known it. We are not arguing that these changes
> should not occur. We are merely saying that if and when they do, the
> institution may fail and need to be reconstructed according to a
> different model.[3]

Adult bonding through equality and reciprocal trust is a new model
for marriage. Equality as a foundation for trust and shared meaning
implies a wholly different mode of relating than does dominance
based on property rights and the social privileges of male suprem-
acy.

While equality seems promising as a new mode of relating in
adult bonding, the changes implied for married and family life seem
overwhelming. An individual couple cannot forge a way of their
own, a new model for daily life. The discontinuity and lack of
traditional supports are naturally accompanied by fears of disintegration. For this reason, couples must learn how to establish a new
symbolic connection to a larger meaning system, beyond the legal or
social institution of marriage as it now exists. Establishing a symbolic connection to self and to the human community is essential for
healing problems of basic trust.

Couples in distress cannot become immediately responsible for
generating their own ideal images for trust and companionship.
They need to be connected both to their own symbolic reality
(through dreams, ritual, art, work and play) and to a community of

like-minded people. Ideally, this community will carry a larger meaning system—a spiritual context for human development—as well as the day-to-day emotional support needed for change.

Assisting the members of a couple in remembering and recording dreams, in increasing their respect for imaginative thinking and their ability to act spontaneously (intuitively), and in expanding their knowledge of mythic symbols are activities essential for successful therapy. These activities are furthered through assigning reading outside of sessions, referring to dreams and networking with groups that are learning or re-learning symbolic modes. Developing a symbolic connection to self and humanity leads to both greater knowledge about the human life cycle and greater hope for the "working through" of conflictual struggles in the process of bonded relationship.

Another way to understand the importance of the symbolic context for vitality in human relationship is to see it as the foundation of psychological activity in the "roots" of living form. Robert Jay Lifton talks about the development of a "grounded imagination" as essential to healthy living in this time of cultural discontinuity.[4] Based on his work with holocaust survivors and contemporary social radicals, Lifton insists that the feeling of vitality and health (or wholeness) rests on our ability to experience the images of self—temporal, spatial and emotional—as intact. The "grounding" of our images of self depends, in turn, on our being able to connect those images to personal and collective history, both biological and social. Lifton further suggests that conscious mentation is a relatively conservative or limited form of thinking in comparison to unconscious mentation. In order to ground or connect unconscious imagination to conscious thinking, a person must develop links or connections between the powerful formative suggestions of dreams or intuition and the daily activities of social and biological reality. Lifton believes that our forgetting of dreams is a product of the constriction of imagination, of a sort of "numbing" or "tuning out" of our fuller thought processes.

If dreams are our most radical and complex thoughts, then our ability to use them depends on our readiness to integrate symbolic images into ordinary waking experience in the interpersonal world. The reluctance of many people to "believe" their dreams and to imagine themselves beyond the immediate confines of time and space can be countered through a therapeutic and instructive process. Lifton reports on a research project in which he taught people to make connections between a waking problem and a dream response:

It consists of focusing, during the moments just before sleep, upon an immediate life struggle bound up with personal conflict and then "willing" a dream that will address that struggle. In the case of the research subjects the images to be focused upon connect with a dominant theme of an interview being completed. The dreams themselves, of course, vary enormously. But through their associations we have consistently encountered strongly prospective patterns. The dream images, though they are usually quite removed in content from the dreamer's concept of his or her impasse, may nonetheless lead by way of associations toward altered perspectives, forms beyond the impasse.[5]

Couples need to develop the ability to ground their dreams and imaginary thoughts (such as intuitive inspirations) in the daily tasks of living. In order to do this, they will need to develop a symbolic context for understanding unconscious thought. An immediately accessible one is through world religions and mythic systems as expressed in a variety of ritual or other cultural forms. Developing a context for using imaginative or symbolic thought results in increased vitality—through the experience of an intact self—and in increased hopefulness about trusting the processes of communication and imagination to generate solutions to conflict. Lifton writes:

In my work I have begun to make distinctions between relatively unconnected imagery and what I call "grounded imagination." Especially strong in the innovator, grounded imagination has roots in a person's living forms; and these roots permit a certain amount of freedom in imagining outward, so to speak, toward new (or new combinations of) images and original forms. The assumption here is that no form can be entirely new but must have imaginative grounding in older ones.[6]

The grounding of imagination in daily life and personal history is an especially exciting endeavor to form new connection in a couple relationship. The members of the couple can feel connected to self, other and human community by unifying daily conscious and unconscious imagery and experience. The symbolic context or symbolic connection, through a shared meaning system of the couple and other couples who are bonding through equality, provides a foundation for felt continuity in a disintegrating society. Furthermore, this kind of symbolic continuity that is grounded in social reality leads to new forms of social reality and human connection beyond the couple.

Our system of revitalization and reconnection in couple relating begins with confronting loss. The shock of separation, experienced as spatial, temporal and emotional loss of self, propels the members of a couple into a re-evaluation of self and other. In the process of this re-evaluation, we stress the activities and thought forms that engender greater equality and mutuality. These are rooted in brother-sister archetypal imagery and in the modes and rituals of peer play, as well as in the intuition of the hag's voice. Imaginative grounding in new symbolic forms for mutual sharing, reciprocal trust and equality is then extended to an experience of a larger symbolic context.

The ability to live in a vital and connected relationship of adult love seems to depend on weaving a fabric of symbolic connections beyond the couple and beyond the individuals. Through these connections to a larger community and a shared symbolic system, individuals can foster an ongoing process of imagining outward, of moving beyond themselves. Ultimately this process seems to result in the establishment of trust in something "beyond" oneself to sustain the individual through personal losses, discontinuities and disintegrations.

In practical terms, this means that daily life includes a faith in the minor rebirths of meaning that occur through the temporary loss and re-establishment of trust. The environment of interpersonal trust expands from personal experience to communal and symbolic continuity. This is the larger goal and ideal that underlies our work in the microcosm of couple therapy.

Appendix A

Gawain and the Lady Ragnell

(From *The Maid of the North and Other Folktale Heroines*)

Long ago, in the days of King Arthur, the finest knight in all Britain was the king's nephew Gawain. He was, by reputation, the bravest in battle, the wisest, the most courteous, the most compassionate, and the most loyal to his king.

One day in late summer, Gawain was with Arthur and the knights of the court at Carlisle in the north. The king returned from the day's hunting looking so pale and shaken that Gawain followed him at once to his chamber.

"What has happened, my lord?" asked Gawain with concern.

Arthur sat down heavily. "I had a very strange encounter in Inglewood forest . . . I hardly know what to make of it." And he related to Gawain what had occurred.

"Today I hunted a great white stag," said Arthur. "The stag at last escaped me and I was alone, some distance from my men. Suddenly a tall, powerful man appeared before me with sword upraised."

"And you were unarmed!"

"Yes. I had only my bow and a dagger in my belt. He threatened to kill me," Arthur went on. "And he swung his sword as though he meant to cut me down on the spot! Then he laughed horribly and said he would give me one chance to save my life."

"Who was this man?" cried Gawain. "Why should he want to kill you?"

"He said his name was Sir Gromer, and he sought revenge for the loss of his northern lands."

"A chieftain from the north!" exclaimed Gawain. "But what is this one chance he spoke of?"

"I gave him my word I would meet him one year from today, unarmed, at the same spot, with the answer to a question!" said Arthur.

Gawain started to laugh, but stopped at once when he saw Arthur's face. "A question! Is it a riddle? And one year to find the answer? That should not be hard!"

"If I can bring him the true answer to the question, 'What is it that women most desire, above all else?' my life will be spared." Arthur scowled. "He is sure I will fail. It must be a foolish riddle that no one can answer."

"My lord, we have one year to search the kingdom for answers," said Gawain confidently. "I will help you. Surely one of the answers will be the right one."

"No doubt you are right—someone will know the answer." Arthur looked more cheerful. "The man is mad, but a chieftain will keep his word."

For the next twelve months, Arthur and Gawain asked the question from

159

one corner of the kingdom to the other. Then at last the appointed day drew near. Although they had many answers, Arthur was worried.

"With so many answers to choose from, how do we know which is the right one?" he asked in despair. "Not one of them has the ring of truth."

A few days before he was to meet Sir Gromer, Arthur rode out alone through the golden gorse and purple heather. The track led upward toward a grove of great oaks. Arthur, deep in thought, did not look up until he reached the edge of the oak wood. When he raised his head, he pulled up suddenly in astonishment.

Before him was a grotesque woman. She was almost as wide as she was high, her skin was mottled green, and spikes of weedlike hair covered her head. Her face seemed more animal than human.

The woman's eyes met Arthur's fearlessly. "You are Arthur the king," she said in a harsh, croaking voice. "In two days' time you must meet Sir Gromer with the answer to a question."

Arthur turned cold with fear. He stammered, "Yes . . . yes . . . that is true. Who are you? How did you know of this?"

"I am the Lady Ragnell. Sir Gromer is my stepbrother. You haven't found the true answer, have you?"

"I have many answers," Arthur replied curtly. "I do not see how my business concerns you." He gathered up the reins, eager to be gone.

"You do not have the right answer." Her certainty filled him with a sense of doom. The harsh voice went on, "But I know the answer to Sir Gromer's question."

Arthur turned back in hope and disbelief. "You do? Tell me the true answer to his question, and I will give you a large bag of gold."

"I have no use for gold," she said coldly.

"Nonsense, my good woman. With gold you can buy anything you want!" He hesitated a moment, for the huge, grotesque face with cool, steady eyes unnerved him. He went on hurriedly, "What is it you want? Jewelry? Land? Whatever you want I will pay you—that is, if you truly have the right answer."

"I know the answer. I promise you that!" She paused. "What I demand in return is that the knight Gawain become my husband."

There was a moment of shocked silence. Then Arthur cried, "Impossible! You ask the impossible, woman!"

She shrugged and turned to leave.

"Wait, wait a moment!" Rage and panic overwhelmed him, but he tried to speak reasonably.

"I offer you gold, land, jewels. I cannot give you my nephew. He is his own man. He is not mine to give!"

"I did not ask you to *give* me the knight Gawain," she rebuked him. "If Gawain himself agrees to marry me, I will give you the answer. Those are my terms."

"Impossible!" he sputtered. "I could not bring him such a proposal."

"If you should change your mind, I will be here tomorrow," said she, and disappeared into the oak woods.

Shaken from the weird encounter, Arthur rode homeward at a slow pace.

"Save my own life at Gawain's expense? Never!" he thought. "Loathsome woman! I could not even speak of it to Gawain."

But the afternoon air was soft and sweet with birdsong, and the fateful meeting with Sir Gromer weighed on him heavily. He was torn by the terrible choice facing him.

Gawain rode out from the castle to meet the king. Seeing Arthur's pale, strained face, he exclaimed, "My Lord! Are you ill? What has happened?"

"Nothing . . . nothing at all." But he could not keep silent long. "The colossal impudence of the woman! A monster, that's what she is! That creature, daring to give me terms!"

"Calm yourself, uncle," Gawain said patiently. "What woman? Terms for what?"

Arthur sighed. "She knows the answer to the question. I didn't intend to tell you."

"Why not? Surely that's good news! What is the answer?"

"She will not tell me until her terms are met," said the king heavily. "But I assure you, I refuse to consider her proposal!"

Gawain smiled. "You talk in riddles yourself, uncle. Who is this woman who claims to know the answer? What is her proposal?"

Seeing Gawain's smiling, expectant face, Arthur at first could not speak. Then, with his eyes averted, the king told Gawain the whole story, leaving out no detail.

"The Lady Ragnell is Sir Gromer's stepsister? Yes, I think she would know the right answer," Gawain said thoughtfully. "How fortunate that I will be able to save your life!"

"No! I will not let you sacrifice yourself!" Arthur cried.

"It is my choice and my decision," Gawain answered. "I will return with you tomorrow and agree to the marriage—on condition that the answer she supplies is the right one to save your life."

Early the following day, Gawain rode out with Arthur. But not even meeting the loathsome lady face to face could shake his resolve. Her proposal was accepted.

Gawain bowed courteously. "If on the morrow your answer saves the king's life, we will be wed."

On the fateful morning, Gawain watched the king stow a parchment in his saddlebag. "I'll try all these answers first," said Arthur.

They rode together for the first part of the journey. Then Arthur, unarmed as agreed, rode on alone to Inglewood to meet Sir Gromer.

The tall, powerful chieftain was waiting, his broadsword glinting in the sun.

Arthur read off one answer, then another, and another. Sir Gromer shook his head in satisfaction.

"No, you have not the right answer!" he said raising his sword high. "You've failed, and now—"

"Wait!" Arthur cried. "I have one more answer. What a woman desires above all else is the power of sovereignty—the right to exercise her own will."

With a loud oath the man dropped his sword. "You did not find that answer by yourself!" he shouted. "My cursed stepsister, Ragnell, gave it to you. Bold, interfering hussy! I'll run her through with my sword . . . I'll lop off her head . . . " Turning, he plunged into the forest, a string of horrible curses echoing behind him.

Arthur rode back to where Gawain waited with the monstrous Ragnell. They returned to the castle in silence. Only the grotesque Lady Ragnell seemed in good spirits.

The news spread quickly throughout the castle. Gawain, the finest knight in the land, was to marry this monstrous creature! Some tittered and laughed at the spectacle; others said the Lady Ragnell must possess very great lands and estates; but mostly there was stunned silence.

Arthur took his nephew aside nervously. "Must you go through with it at once? A postponement perhaps?"

Gawain looked at him steadily. "I gave my promise, my lord. The Lady Ragnell's answer saved your life. Would you have me—"

"Your loyalty makes me ashamed! Of course you cannot break your word." And Arthur turned away.

The marriage took place in the abbey. Afterward, with Gawain and the lady sitting at the high dais table beside the king and queen, the strange wedding feast began.

"She takes the space of two women on the chair," muttered the knight Gareth. "Poor Gawain!"

"I would not marry such a creature for all the land in Christendom!" answered his companion.

An uneasy silence settled on the hall. Only the monstrous Lady Ragnell displayed good spirits and good appetite. Throughout the long day and evening, Gawain remained pleasant and courteous. In no way did his manner toward his strange bride show other than kind attention.

The wedding feast drew to a close. Gawain and his bride were conducted to their chamber and were at last alone.

The Lady Ragnell gazed at her husband thoughtfully.

"You have kept your promise well and faithfully," she observed.

Gawain inclined his head. "I could not do less, my lady."

"You've shown neither revulsion nor pity," she said. After a pause she went on, "Come now, we are wedded! I am waiting to be kissed."

Gawain went to her at once and kissed her. When he stepped back, there stood before him a slender young woman with gray eyes and a serene, smiling face.

His scalp tingled in shock. "What manner of sorcery is this?" he cried hoarsely.

"Do you prefer me in this form?" she smiled and turned slowly in a full circle.

But Gawain backed away warily. "I . . . yes . . . of course . . . but . . . I don't understand . . . " For this sudden evidence of sorcery, with its unknown powers, made him confused and uneasy.

"My stepbrother, Sir Gromer, had always hated me," said the Lady Ragnell. "Unfortunately, through his mother, he has a knowledge of sorcery, and so he changed me into a monstrous creature. He said I must live in that shape until I could persuade the greatest knight in Britain to willingly choose me for his bride. He said it would be an impossible condition to meet!"

"Why did he hate you so cruelly?"

Her lips curled in amusement. "He thought me bold and unwomanly because I defied him. I refused his commands both for my property and my person."

Gawain said with admiration, "You won the 'impossible' condition he set, and now his evil spell is broken!"

"Only in part." Her clear gray eyes held his. "You have a choice, my dear Gawain, which way I will be. Would you have me in this, my own shape, at night and my former ugly shape by day? Or would you have me grotesque at night in our chamber, and my own shape in the castle by day? Think carefully before you choose."

Gawain was silent only a moment. He knelt before her and touched her hand.

"It is a choice I cannot make, my dear Ragnell. It concerns you. Whatever you choose to be—fair by day or fair by night—I will willingly abide by it."

Ragnell released a long, deep breath. The radiance in her face overwhelmed him.

"You have answered well, dearest Gawain, for your answer has broken Gromer's evil spell completely. The last condition he set has been met! For he said that if, after marriage to the greatest knight in Britain, my husband freely gave me the power of choice, the power to exercise my own free will, the wicked enchantment would be broken forever."

Thus, in wonder and in joy, began the marriage of Gawain and the Lady Ragnell.

Appendix B

Psychosexual Assessment

This assessment may be carried out with the couple together or with the individuals separately. It can be worked into the process of meeting with the clients initially or it can be done explicitly in a separate meeting. When sexual difficulties have been singled out as the presenting problem, a special session devoted only to psychosexual assessment is usually helpful.

If sexual difficulties are or seem to be prominent in a couple's history, you should spend some time with each member of the couple individually so that each person may disclose privately any fears or behaviors that might be too difficult to bring up in the co-therapy session. Remember, however, if you are working with the couple on an ongoing basis, you should encourage the disclosure of secrets in the co-therapy session. There should be no sense of a private arrangement between one of the therapists and one member of the couple.

The following sets of concerns may be tackled in any order and in any manner, either as a part of a general interview session or explicitly as separate concerns. As much as possible, we insist on behavioral descriptions rather than qualitative judgments. For example, a "good sex life" may mean anything from frequent sex to a mutual agreement to constrain the sexual relationship to only certain kinds of sexual involvement. Find out explicitly what people mean when they indicate preferences or difficulties. If you are meeting with the couple in a co-therapy session to assess sexual functioning, it is preferable to use the empathy interview with each individual in order to get complete descriptive details.

Before taking a sexual history, create an atmosphere for frankness and lowered anxiety. You may do this by introducing the assessment as a "structured experience" and by asking questions in a clinical manner. Indicating that most people feel somewhat anxious and embarrassed by talking directly about their sex life will usually lower tensions. Perceived sexual dysfunction is generally very difficult to discuss. If you perceive the possibility of a sexual dysfunction such as primary impotence, you may need to draw out the individual in a separate interview. Acknowledging the anxiety of self-esteem and giving a clear context of "no blame" will increase the likelihood of exploring the problem descriptively and moving on to further development. As a therapist, you must convey both objective empathy and a sense of security or expertise.

1) Sexual Problem

What does each couple member perceive as the sexual problem between them? Each person should describe the perceived problem in terms of behaviors—i.e., exactly what is said and done. Even reports of how often a couple has sexual contact may differ for each member of the couple. One member may report, for example, that they have sex two or three times a week and the other member reports a grand total of twice a month. Each person has a personal context for experiencing both the problem and the sexual history of the relationship. This personal context will shape and color the actual report in the session.

2) Sexual Contract

What agreement do the partners have about how often and under what circumstances they will have sex? Where does contact usually occur? Who initiates? How is desire for contact communicated? Does each person understand the "come-on" of the other? How is refusal communicated? What is the typical routine of sexual contact? Under what circumstances does this routine vary? Sometimes there is a hidden contract that only one member of the couple should have sexual pleasure—usually the man—as pleasure is implicitly "exchanged" for something else (such as financial support) within the couple.

Couples have very different kinds of contracts concerning sexual intimacy. Sometimes there has been an "agreement" (conscious or unconscious) that sexual contact can take place outside the relationship under certain circumstances, for example, when one member is out of town. Sex may be used for dominance (control) or as an exchange for a variety of other permissions (e.g., in exchange for expensive material buying). During the assessment, no judgment should be made about the current contract; rather, it should be examined and understood as clearly as possible. For example, one of the therapists may explicitly state something like, "You and your husband both seem to agree that he can be promiscuous in exchange for your being able to pursue your creative interests independently."

Remember to keep in mind preferences for fetishes and masturbation as part of a couple's sexual contract. At times, these kinds of preferences are missed by therapists who have in mind their own particular standards for sexual relating.

3) Attractiveness

Find out how attracted each member is to the other. You may do this by asking explicit questions or by observing unobtrusively. You may or may not want to share your observations with the couple.

When assessing attractiveness, look for congruence between each person's personality and appearance. Look also for general congruence between the "power of appearance" in the two people. Are they both powerful in appearance—or only one?

Talk about romance. What is romantic and stimulating for each person? How is romance evoked? What situations and/or tools accompany it—e.g., movies, sexual books, dress, vibrators, contexts, etc.?

What is the typical "identity state" for sexual attraction in each partner? Does the person identify with being heroic, child-like, maternal, playmate, etc., during sexual attraction?

Sometimes it is helpful to see photographs of the couple during their early relationship, when presumedly they felt highly attracted to one another. You can explore the changes with them in terms of what each partner sees then and now.

4) Family of Origin

What were parental communications about sex and love? How were these expressed in the original family? How was sex discussed? How would an outsider know what was going on with the parents sexually—i.e., what did the parents *do* to show their sexual feelings? What was the general sexual climate in the family of origin: open, stimulating, closed, suppressed, private, joyful, depressed, etc.?

Who was the main source of sexual information during childhood: peers, teachers, parents? What images were used to convey sexual meanings in the family, at school, in church, in the neighborhood?

What is each partner's current knowledge of sexual relating? What is the state of each partner's physiological, contraceptive, psychological, anatomical and interpersonal knowledge? Who does each person go to with questions about sexual functioning in the current life situation? (Often women are uninformed about female sexuality per se although they may know a great deal about male responsiveness.)

5) Sexual History

This is usually the most important part of the interview from the point of view of psychodynamics. Determine each person's memories of sexual milestones:
  first kiss
  playing doctor
  peer sharing
  nocturnal emission
  masturbation
  menstruation
  hormonal changes in appearance
  dating
  first sexual intimacy
  first intercourse (under what circumstances?)
  first love
  petting
  secret sex
Look especially at the implied or non-rational levels of communication. How much did the person perceive self as "normal" and "regular" in comparison to peers? If the man did not experience intercourse until the age of twenty-one, for example, you should explore the reasons why and his situation, as this is outside of the cultural norm for men. For the woman there is no comparable cultural norm for first intercourse. The woman may have imposed a norm on herself, however, from her peer group and/or parents. The first romantic love and the first sexual encounter will usually create an early context of meaning for what follows.

6) Present Couple Relationship

Ask each partner to recount the history of their relationship from the point of view of romance and sexual intimacy. The following concerns should be focal:
initial meeting
dating history
expectations of each other sexually
first intercourse
secret sex
contraception
differences in sex before and after marriage
honeymoon or first married night
other marriages
children in relation to sexual intimacy
history of pregnancy and postpartum sexuality
goals for the future
fidelity, homosexuality, masturbation
communication of intimate feelings
communication with peer couples
amount and situations (time of day, etc.) of intimacy currently in the
    couple's life

7) Special Constraints

Certain situational factors constrain sexual behavior. Explore with the individuals their own assessments of how, if at all, the following factors may constrain their sexual relating:
physical illness
responsibilities to children or aging parents
job responsibilities
religious injunctions or beliefs
contraceptive problems
alcoholism
use of drugs

8) Sexual Dysfunctions

If you are not familiar with typical sexual dysfunctions (so that you could identify them from description), review the section called "Psychosexual Disorders" in the *Diagnostic and Statistical Manual of Mental Disorders* (Third Edition) of the American Psychiatric Association. The manual has incorporated descriptive categories from research on sexual dysfunction, such as that of Masters and Johnson. These categories review the important presenting problems connected with sexual disturbances. You can ask questions relevant to exploring a dysfunction if you detect it from the psychosexual assessment. Dysfunction is a difficult subject for the client to disclose and should be handled as expertly, as objectively and as empathically as possible.

Appendix C

Developmental Assessment in Context

Two kinds of reflective activity are involved in a developmental assessment: description and analysis. Description concerns the facts, data, impressions (visual and otherwise) and narrative history of the person in life context. Analysis concerns the use of theoretical frames of reference to sort the facts into categories of meaning which are relevant to the work of psychotherapy. Analysis attempts to sort the facts into some kind of more enduring "truth" so that the therapist can establish a symbolic context for the treatment.

The following suggestions for analyzing facts derive from our assumptions about working with couples. My leaning is toward the use of stage developmental theory and a blend of psychodynamic categories for understanding personality functioning. The suggestions here are simply suggestions, and the analysis may be organized in any way that suits the therapist in order to link assessment and treatment.

The line of reasoning is linked as follows:

Presenting Problem (description) — Personal Data (description) — Assessment of Person (analysis) — Assessment of Problem (analysis) — Initial Goals of Treatment — Method of Treatment — Reassessment of Problem (analysis) — Reassessment of Person — etc.

Personal data and impressions are gathered in the context of the presenting problem. These are analyzed into a framework of meaning (usually development and personality) within the life history and context of the person. From this the therapist conceives of the "problem" as a psychotherapeutic project. Goals are then formulated and often a timetable is developed. Decisions are made about the method of treatment, given the problem and personality of the clients and the desirable goals. These may be modified or accepted as originally envisioned. In essence, the process of assessment is circular and ongoing; yet it must take place initially as thoroughly as possible in order for psychotherapy to be a shared project. It is only through the specification of an assessment that client and therapist(s) can agree on their reasons for meeting together and engaging in the work of therapy.

The following categories of assessment provide some guidelines for carrying out this process through the interview format. The use of psychological tests is not included because we do not use such tests (even of the Jungian typology sort) in assessing people for couple therapy. If extensive individual assessment becomes necessary, we generally have already assigned people to individual therapy. The categories listed here can be understood as guiding concepts for assessing individual functioning within the couple.

Identity information: age, ethnic background, social class, work or career, educational status, referral source and current living situation (environment and other people who live in that environment).

Appearance: general health, height, weight, style of dress, attention to grooming, etc., impressions conveyed by appearance (such as "college student"); impressions of self through body movements, speech and gesture (e.g., hopeful, energetic, tired, weak, etc.).

Presenting problem: summarize, in the words of the client(s), the complaints and/or concerns which are presented as the reason for self- or other-referral for psychotherapeutic treatment; use the client's words and images for describing the presenting problems, and do not embellish with psychological terms unless the client does so.

Family of origin and developmental history: to an appropriate degree, collect in your mind the facts of family history (e.g., place of birth and rearing, major losses, major moves, etc.) from the client's story. Review main events from school years and sibling relationships.

Medical and psychiatric history: dates and reported causes of all hospitalizations, psychiatric treatments and history of drug and alcohol abuse. (This information should be elicited in the context of general questions about the past.)

Current relationship life: facts about current family and work life—children, living relatives, friends, colleagues; establish a sense of the interpersonal fabric or network of the client's daily life.

Assessment of client's personality and development: analyze the typical defense mechanisms as indicators of current developmental functioning (e.g., using Vaillant's hierarchy of defense mechanisms from *Adaptation to Life*); analyze characteristic cognitive patterns as indicators of cognitive development (e.g., using Piaget's forms of thought operations, Loevinger's ego development stages or Perry's forms of intellectual reasoning); analyze characteristic moral and ethical reasoning (e.g., using Loevinger, Kohlberg or Carol Gilligan) to assess the kind of motivation the client brings for change—i.e., what naturally motivates this person to change: material rewards? social approval? self-fulfillment?

Assess overall integration of the personality in the light of typical functioning under anxiety-provoking conditions. How does this person defend against the anxiety aroused in the therapy situation? How vulnerable is the person to disintegration under pressure? What is the "style" of personality that is expressed in anxiety management—e.g., hysterical, obsessive, compulsive, depressive, etc. The style of personality can also be characterized by images from the complexes, that is, the hag or bully. These images may be transitory or enduring. The conscious personality may contrast with unconscious style.

Assessment of the problem: in the light of all the data collected and the assessment of the client's personality and development, what is your assessment of the problem to be treated in psychotherapy? Formulate your ideas in terms which lead directly to therapeutic interventions—in terms of meaning, motivation and empathy. The assessment of the problem should be clearly and cleanly stated in a few sentences. The problem for therapeutic intervention is delineated from a larger universe of problems presented by the client in life context. Not all of these problems will be treated in a single therapeutic intervention, or even in extensive analysis of many years.

Goals of treatment: in the light of the data, the assessment of the client and the assessment of the problem, what are the goals or anticipated outcomes of your therapeutic intervention? Give short-term and long-term goals with a time frame. This statement of goals may include future interventions (e.g., personality restructuring) that will not be a part of the immediate psychotherapy.

Treatment agreement: the goals of treatment are translated back into the client's language and into the context of the presenting problem. These goals are then stated to the client in terms which are clear and empathic with the client's situation. Agreement must be reached between client and therapist as to the purpose of their meetings together.

Assessment of the treatment: the circular recapitulation of the assessment process for ongoing reassessment of problem, person and goals.

NOTES

CW—*The Collected Works of C. G. Jung*

1   The Use of Stories in Psychotherapy

1. Helen Swick Perry, *Psychiatrist of America: The Life of Harry Stack Sullivan*, p. 334.

2. Thomas S. Kuhn, *The Structure of Scientific Revolutions*.

3. For a discussion of Winnicott's concept of "continuity of being," see Mary Davis and David Wallbridge, *Boundary and Space: An Introduction to the Work of D. W. Winnicott*.

4. John Bowlby, *Attachment and Loss*, vol. 1.

5. Peggy Sanday, *Female Power and Male Dominance: On the Origins of Sexual Inequality*, p. 5.

6. Nancy Chodorow, "Being and Doing: A Cross-cultural Examination of the Socialization of Males and Females," in V. Gornick and B. K. Moran, eds., *Woman in Sexist Society: Studies in Power and Powerlessness*, pp. 290-291.

7. There are several versions of the story of Sir Gawain and the Lady Ragnell, the most famous of which is a variation told by the Wife of Bath in Chaucer's *Canterbury Tales*, written around 1478. Chaucer's version is quite different from the apparently original Middle English folk ballad, *The Weddynge of Sir Gawen and Dame Ragnell*, recorded about 1450 and preserved in a manuscript of the early sixteenth century. The same story is told, with some variations, in the ballad *The Marriage of Sir Gawain*, preserved in Bishop Percy's folio manuscript of the mid-seventeenth century. Another version is told in Gower's *Confessio amantis* as the "Tale of Florent."
    The version I use is based in part on my experience in working with couples, but in the main is taken from a collection edited by Ethel Johnston Phelps called *The Maid of the North and Other Folktale Heroines* (presented in the appendix in its entirety). One notable difference between Phelps's version and the original (which appears in Donald Sands, ed., *Middle English Verse Romances*) is Ragnell's statement that Gawain must be willing to marry her. In the medieval ballad, Ragnell simply asks that Gawain be given to her in marriage. She says: "Thou must graunt me a knight to wed / His name is Sir Gawen. / And suche covenaunt I wolle make thee / But thorowe mine answere thy lif saved be" (p. 333). She does not mention that the choice to wed her should be Gawain's. This is the only significant difference between the two versions, regarding the interpretation I have given.

8. C. S. Lewis, *The Allegory of Love*.

9. David Gutmann, "The Cross-cultural Perspective: Notes Towards a Comparative Psychology of Aging," in J. Birren and K. W. Schaie, eds., *Handbook of the Psychology of Aging*.

2   Feminism and the Psychology of C.G. Jung

1. Two examples of feminist critiques of Jung's psychology are Carol Christ, "Some Comments on Jung, Jungians and the Study of Women," pp. 68-69, and Naomi Goldenberg, "Jung and Feminism," pp. 443-449. pp. 443-449.

2. Jung, "Mind and Earth," *Civilization in Transition,* CW 10, par. 81.

3. See, for example, Toni Wolff, "Structural Forms of the Feminine Psyche." (This is a monograph not easily available in English outside of Jung Institute libraries, but a good summary appears in Donald Lee Williams, *Border Crossings: A Psychological Perspective on Carlos Castaneda's Path of Knowledge,* pp. 119-122.)

4. Jung, *Aion,* CW 9ii, par. 27.

5. Jung, "Mind and Earth," *Civilization in Transition,* CW 10, par. 81.

6. Jung, "Concerning Rebirth," *The Archetypes and the Collective Unconscious,* CW 9i, par. 223.

7. I would like to thank Demaris Wehr, Ph.D. for her insights and contributions to the analysis of Jung's concept of the animus. She provided both the central ideas and the quotations from Jung's work on the animus concept, but I am responsible for the discussion presented here and accountable for any flaws in it.

8. For a discussion of the domain and concepts of feminist therapy, see A. M. Brodsky and R. Hare-Mustin, eds., *Women and Psychotherapy: An Assessment of Research and Practice.*

9. I. K. Broverman, S. R. Vogel, D. M. Broverman, R. E. Clarkson and P. S. Rosenkrantz, "Sex-role Stereotypes: A Current Appraisal," pp. 59-78.

10. I. K. Broverman, D. M. Broverman, R. E. Clarkson, P. S. Rosenkrantz and S. R. Vogel, "Sex-role Stereotypes and Clinical Judgments of Mental Health," pp. 1-7.

11. See, for example, Alice Eagly, "Gender and Social Influences: A Social Psychological Analysis," pp. 971-981.

12. See the discussion of feminism and Jung's psychology in Polly Young-Eisendrath and Florence Wiedemann, *Female Authority.*

13. Anthony Stevens, *Archetypes: A Natural History of the Self,* pp. 174-209.

14. R. T. Hare-Mustin, J. Maracek, A. G. Kaplan and N. Liss-Levinson, "The Rights of Clients, the Responsibilities of Therapists," pp. 3-16.

15. Jung, "Some Aspects of Modern Psychotherapy," *The Practice of Psychotherapy,* CW 16, par. 53.

16. Bowlby, *Attachment and Loss,* vol. 1.

17. Jung, "Medicine and Psychotherapy," *The Practice of Psychotherapy,* CW 16, par. 208.

18. Stevens, *Archetypes,* p. 89.

19. Jung himself refers to them as both complexes and archetypes; I have found it most useful to think of these sub-personalities as complexes.

To speak in terms of archetypes of animus or anima, one must assume that a particular archetypal image is associated with each of these sub-personalities. The archetypal images of masculine and feminine principles cannot be attached to animus and anima because gender differentiation varies according to culture and social groups. Conceptualizing the animus and anima as the "underside" or excluded aspects of an individual's gender identity allows us to view these aspects differentially as they evolve developmentally and through social-cultural influences.

20. Carolyn W. Sherif, "Needed Concepts in the Study of Gender Identity," p. 376.

21. See the chapters on animus development in Young-Eisendrath and Wiedemann, *Female Authority.*

22. Jane Loevinger, *Ego Development.*

23. Animus development in terms of psychopathology is discussed in detail in Young-Eisendrath and Wiedemann, *Female Authority.*

24. See Loevinger, *Ego Development.* The impulsive stage of ego development is characterized by pre-operational thought and impulsive acting out. There is little differentiation of feeling, thought and action and the self is understood primarily in terms of deeds. Consequences of actions cannot be anticipated and basic reward-punishment orientation has not been internalized. The self-protective stage is characterized by concrete and stereotyped thinking, and by wishing and fearing. Responsibility and blame are externalized, but a basic reward-punishment sequence is understood. Motivations are organized around avoiding pain and trouble and seeking pleasure. Interpersonal relating is characterized by ambivalence and opportunism. Hostility and aggression are both expressed and projected as frequent occurrences in intimate relating. The self is experienced in terms of action, foresight and anticipation of consequences.

3 C.G. Jung and Harry Stack Sullivan

1. Harold Searles, "Phases of Patient-Therapist Interaction in the Psychotherapy of Schizophrenia," pp. 538-539.

4 Enacting the Complex: Hag, Hero and Bully

1. Geneen Roth, *Feeding the Hungry Heart,* p. 3.

2. See Carolyn W. Sherif, "Needed Concepts in the Study of Gender Identity," pp. 375-398. Sherif says: "Recent comparative analyses of gender categories and norms by anthropologists (Quinn, 1977; Whyte, 1978) make it ... clear that the sociocultural basis for gender is not 'unitary' or simple, naive perception. To quote Rosaldo (1980), gender is a 'complex product of a variety of social forces' that differ in different societies and historical periods. Whyte (1978) asserts that there is no universal social category 'women' apart from a particular cultural-historical context." (p. 377)

3. Bowlby, *Attachment and Loss,* vol. 1.

4. Albert Alvarez, *Life After Marriage: Love in an Age of Divorce*, pp. 117-118.

5. Stevens, *Archetypes*, pp. 174-209.

6. Ibid., p. 187.

7. Ibid., p. 189.

8. Ibid.

9. Ibid., p. 191.

5 Embracing the Hag in Middle Life

1. S. H. Budman, M. J. Bennett and M. J. Wisneski, "An Adult Developmental Model of Short-term Group Psythotherapy," in Simon Budman, ed., *Forms of Brief Therapy*, pp. 305-342.

2. E. Jaques, "Death and the Mid-life Crisis," pp. 502-514.

3. D. G. Gutmann,"Parenthood: A Key to the Comparative Study of the Life Cycle," in N. Datan and L. Ginsberg, eds., *Developmental Psychology*.

4. Jessie Bernard, *The Future of Marriage*.

5. Jean Piaget, *The Moral Judgment of the Child*.

6. Arthur Coleman and Libby Coleman, *Earth Father, Sky Father: The Changing Concept of Fathering*, p. 73.

7. John Money, "Differentiation of Gender Identity," p. 20.

8. Ibid., p. 13.

9. H. F. Harlow and M. K. Harlow, "Learning to Love," pp. 244-272.

10. Margaret Mead, *Growing up in New Guinea, The South Seas: Studies of Adolescence and Sex in Three Primitive Societies*, vol. 2.

11. Coleman and Coleman, *Earth Father, Sky Father*, p. 170.

6 Methodology in Couple Therapy

1. Thomas Allen is Associate Professor of Counseling Psychology, Graduate Institute of Education, Washington University, St. Louis.

2. Carl J. Sager, *Marriage Contracts and Couple Therapy*.

3. William Goodheart, "Theory of Analytic Interaction," pp. 2-39.

8 Conclusion: Vitality through Connection

1. Robert Jay Lifton, *The Life of the Self: Toward a New Psychology*, p. 35.

2. Philip Blumstein and Pepper Schwartz, *American Couples*.

3. Ibid., p. 320.

4. Lifton, *The Life of the Self*, p. 101.

5. Ibid., p. 103.

6. Ibid., p. 101.

Bibliography

Select Reading for Jung and Sullivan

Jung, C.G. "Definitions." *Psychological Types,* CW 6. (See General References below for publication details of Jung's *Collected Works,* referred to as CW.)

——. "On the Psychology of the Unconscious." *Two Essays on Analytical Psychology,* CW 7.

——. "On Psychic Energy," "On the Nature of the Psyche" and "The Transcendent Function." *The Structure and Dynamics of the Psyche,* CW 8.

——. "Conscious, Unconscious and Individuation." *The Archetypes and the Collective Unconscious,* CW 9i.

——. "Problems of Modern Psychotherapy," "Medicine and Psychotherapy" and "The Aims of Psychotherapy." *The Practice of Psychotherapy,* CW 16.

Sullivan, H.S. *Conceptions of Modern Psychiatry,* W.W. Norton, New York, 1953.

——. *The Interpersonal Theory of Psychiatry.* W.W. Norton, New York, 1953.

——. *The Psychiatric Interview.* W.W. Norton, New York, 1954.

——. *The Fusion of Psychiatry and Social Science.* W.W. Norton, New York, 1964.

Recommended Biographies of Jung and Sullivan

Brome, Vincent. *C.G. Jung: Man and Myth.* Atheneum, New York, 1978.

Perry, Helen S. *Psychiatrist of America: The Life of Harry Stack Sullivan.* Harvard University Press, Cambridge, 1982.

Von Franz, Marie-Louise. *C.G. Jung: His Myth in Our Time.* G.P. Putnam's Sons, New York, 1975.

Select Reading for Psychodrama Techniques

Blatner, H.A. *Acting-in: Practical Applications of Psychodramatic Methods.* Springer, New York, 1973.

Haskell, M.R. *Socioanalysis: Self Direction via Sociometry and Psychodrama.* Anderson, Ritchie and Simon, Los Angeles, 1975.

Moreno, J.L. *Psychodrama,* vol. 1. Beacon House, New York, 1972.

Moreno, J.T. "A Survey of Psychodrama Techniques." *Group Psychotherapy and Psychodrama,* vol. 12 (1959).

General References

Alvarez, Albert. *Life After Marriage.* Simon and Schuster, New York, 1981.

Bernard, Jessie. *The Future of Marriage.* World, New York, 1972.

Birren, J. and Schaie, K. W., eds. *Handbook of the Psychology of Aging.* Van Nostrand Reinhold, New York, 1977.

Blumstein, Philip and Schwartz, Pepper. *American Couples.* William Morrow and Co., New York, 1983.

Bowlby, John. *Attachment and Loss,* vol. 1. Hogarth Press, London, 1969.

Brodsky, A. M. and Hare-Mustin, R., eds. *Women and Psychotherapy: An Assessment of Research and Practice.* Guilford Press, New York, 1980.

Broverman, I. K., Vogel, S. R., Broverman, D. M., Clarkson, R. E. and Rosenkrantz, P. S. "Sex-role Stereotypes: A Current Appraisal." *Journal of Socal Issues,* vol. 28 (1972).

———, Broverman, D. M., Clarkson, F. E., Rosenkrantz, P. S. and Vogel, S. R. "Sex-role Stereotypes and Clinical Judgments of Mental Health." *Journal of Consulting and Clinical Psychology,* vol. 34 (1970).

Budman, Simon, ed. *Forms of Brief Therapy.* Guilford Press, New York, 1981.

Christ, Carol. "Some Comments on Jung, Jungians and the Study of Women." *Anima,* vol. 3 (1977), no. 2.

Coleman, A. and Coleman, L. *Earth Father, Sky Father: The Changing Concept of Fathering.* Prentice Hall, Englewood Cliffs, N. J., 1981.

Datan, N. and Ginsberg, L., eds. *Developmental Psychology.* Academic Press, New York, 1975.

Davis, Mary and Wallbridge, David. *Boundary and Space: An Introduction to the Work of D. W. Winnicott.* Brunner/Mazel, New York, 1981.

Eagly, Alice. "Gender and Social Influences: A Social Psychological Analysis." *American Psychologist,* vol. 38 (1983).

Gilligan, Carol. *In a Different Voice: Psychological Theory and Women's Development.* Harvard University Press, Cambridge, 1982.

Goldenberg, Naomi. "Jung and Feminism." *Signs: A Journal of Women in Culture and Society,* vol. 2 (1976), no. 2.

Goodheart, W. "Theory of Analytic Interaction." *The San Francisco Jung Institute Library Journal,* vol. 1 (1980).

Gornick, V. and Moran, B. K., eds. *Woman in Sexist Society: Studies in Power and Powerlessness.* Mentor Books, New York, 1971.

Harding, Esther. *The I and the Not-I* (Bollingen Series LXXIX). Princeton University Press, Princeton, 1965.

Hare-Mustin, R. T., Maracek, J., Kaplan, A. G. and Liss-Levinson, N. "The Rights of Clients, the Responsibilities of Therapists." *American Psychologist,* vol. 34 (1979).

Harlow, H. F. and Harlow, M. K. "Learning to Love." *Scientific American,* vol. 54 (1966).

Jaques, E. "Death and the Mid-life Crisis." *International Journal of Psychoanalysis,* vol. 46 (1965).

Jung, C. G. *The Collected Works* (Bollingen Series XX). 20 vols. Trans. R. F. C. Hull. Ed. H. Read, M. Fordham, G. Adler, Wm. McGuire. Princeton University Press, Princeton, 1953-1979.

Kohlberg, L. "Development of Moral Character and Moral Ideology." In M. L. Hoffman and L. W. Hoffman, eds., *Review of Child Development Research,* vol. 1. Russell Sage Foundation, New York, 1964.

Kuhn, T. S. *The Structure of Scientific Revolutions* (2nd edition). University of Chicago Press, Chicago, 1970.

Lewis, C. S. *The Allegory of Love.* Oxford University Press, Oxford, 1936.

Lifton, Robert Jay. *The Life of the Self: Toward a New Psychology.* Basic Books, New York, 1983.

Loevinger, Jane. *Ego Development.* Jossey-Bass, San Francisco, 1976.

Mead, Margaret. *Growing up in New Guinea, The South Seas: Studies of Adolescence and Sex in Three Primitive Societies,* vol. 2. Morrow, New York, 1939.

Money, John. "Differentiation of Gender Identity." *JSAS: Catalogue of Selected Documents in Psychology,* vol. 6 (1976), no. 4.

Perera, Sylvia Brinton. *Descent to the Goddess: A Way of Initiation for Women.* Inner City Books, Toronto, 1981.

Phelps, Ethel J. *The Maid of the North and Other Folktale Heroines.* Holt, Rinehart and Winston, New York, 1981.

Piaget, Jean. *The Moral Judgment of the Child.* Free Press, New York, 1932.

Roth, G. *Feeding the Hungry Heart.* New American Library, New York, 1982.

Sager, C. J. *Marriage Contracts and Couple Therapy.* Brunner/Mazel, New York, 1976.

Sanday, Peggy. *Female Power and Male Dominance: On the Origins of Sexual Inequality.* Cambridge University Press, Cambridge, England, 1981.

Sands, Donald, ed. *Middle English Verse Romances.* Holt, Rinehart and Winston, New York, 1966.

Searles, Harold. "Phases of Patient-Therapist Interaction in the Psychotherapy of Schizophrenia." In *Collected Papers on Schizophrenia and Related Subjects.* International Universities Press, New York, 1965.

Sherif, Carolyn W. "Needed Concepts in the Study of Gender Identity." *Psychology of Women Quarterly,* vol. 6 (1982).

Stevens, Anthony. *Archetypes: A Natural History of the Self.* William Morrow, New York, 1982.

Vaillant, George. *Adaptation to Life.* Boston, Little Brown, 1977.

Williams, Donald Lee. *Border Crossings: A Psychological Perspective on Carlos Castaneda's Path of Knowledge.* Inner City Books, Toronto, 1981.

Wolff, Toni. "Structural Forms of the Feminine Psyche." Herausgeber G. H. Graber, Bern, Switzerland, 1956.

Woodman, Marion. *The Owl Was a Baker's Daughter: Obesity, Anorexia Nervosa and the Repressed Feminine.* Inner City Books, Toronto, 1980.

———. *Addiction to Perfection: The Still Unravished Bride.* Inner City Books, Toronto, 1982.

Young-Eisendrath, P. and Wiedemann, F. *Female Authority.* Forthcoming.

Index

abandonment, fear of, 141
abuse, physical, 119-120, 147-151
adaptation, change in, 20-22, 87
Adler, Alfred, 53-54
affect-laden preconcepts, 48, 56, 58, 63
alchemy, 48
Allen, Thomas, 118
Allen, Woody, 14, 18-19
Alvarez, A., 79-80
Amor and Psyche, 37
androcentrism, 23-24
androgyne, 38-39
anger, 20-22, 78, 85-86, 90-91, 102, 115-116, 119-120
anima: 20, 23-27, 31, 40-41, 45, 61, 81, 86, 173
  as hag, 81-83
  projection of, 24, 91, 100, 103, 127-131
  as soul/Eros, 32
  split, 100-101
animus: 20, 23-27, 31-34, 41, 61, 66, 81, 86-87, 91, 96
  as alien other, 35, 39, 81, 147, 149
  as androgyne, 38-39
  development (stages of), 33-41, 81, 147
  as father, God, patriarch, 35-36, 81
  as Logos/Spirit, 32
  as partner within, 37-38
  projection of, 24, 33, 102, 126-131
  surrender to, 36
  as youth, hero, lover, 36-37
anthropology, 10, 12, 48, 51, 73, 83
anxiety, 54-62, 66, 69, 89, 115, 119, 124, 147-148
archetype/archetypal: 11-14, 23-24, 26, 44-47, 52, 58, 60, 62-63, 65, 70-71, 120, 125-131, 145-146, 154
  definition, 29-31, 44
Archetypes: A Natural History of the Self, 82

Ariadne, 38
Arthur, King, 16-20, 65, 73-75, 77-80, 83, 85
assessment: developmental, 145, 149-152, 168-170
  initial, 114-122, 139, 145
  interpersonal, 117-122
  psychosexual, 140, 164-167
attachment-separation pattern, 10-12, 15, 21, 30-31, 65, 71, 83, 89-90, 94
attitudes, reconstructing, 23-34, 40, 129-131, 153-158
authority, female (*see also* feminine, revaluing), 25-26, 37, 42-43, 70-73, 77-78, 87-92, 99-106, 119, 126-127, 141-142

Bernard, Jessie, 88
bisexuality, 41
Blumstein, Philip, 154-155
Bond, James, 14, 18-19
bonding: adult, 30, 89-90, 98-99, 154
  infant-parent, 10-11, 30, 82, 95
Bowlby, John, 10, 30, 71
breast, good and bad, 57-58
Broverman et al., 25-26
bully: 39-40, 65, 67-68, 85, 91, 93, 98, 102, 116, 129, 141, 146, 154
  identification with, 40, 78-81, 148-152

care-giving: 12-15, 26-27, 65, 70-74, 82, 89
  compulsive, 69-71
  sharing, 76-78, 89-100, 103-106, 122, 128
Chodorow, Nancy, 13
choice, free, 18, 88, 100-102
chum, 50, 64, 90, 151
client assessment, 117-122
Coleman, A. and L., 92, 98-99

179

Friends of the Elkhart Public Library, Inc.

300 SOUTH SECOND STREET ELKHART, IN 46516 (219)522-3333

I want to be a **FRIEND OF THE ELKHART PUBLIC LIBRARY!**

Name _____

Address _____ Phone _____

City _____ Zip _____

☐ $5.00 Individual ☐ $ ____ Gift
☐ $10.00 Family ☐ $200.00 Corporate

**PLEASE MAIL THIS BOOKMARK
WITH YOUR CHECK TO:**

**FRIENDS OF THE ELKHART PUBLIC
LIBRARY, Inc.**
300 South Second Street
Elkhart, Indiana 46516

**CATALOGUE
AND ORDER FORM**

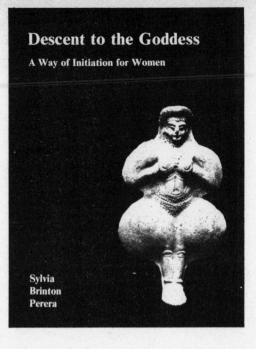

Descent to the Goddess

A Way of Initiation for Women

Sylvia
Brinton
Perera

6. Descent to the Goddess: A Way of Initiation for Women. $10
    Sylvia Brinton Perera (New York). ISBN 0-919123-05-8. 112 pages.

This is a highly original and provocative book about women's freedom and the need for an inner, female authority in a masculine-oriented society.

Combining ancient texts and modern dreams, the author, a practising therapist, presents a way of feminine initiation. Inanna-Ishtar, Sumerian Goddess of Heaven and Earth, journeys into the underworld to Ereshkigal, her dark "sister," and returns. So modern women must descend from their old role-determined behavior into the depths of their instinct and image patterns, to find anew the Great Goddess and restore her values to modern culture.

Men too will be interested in this book, both for its revelations of women's essential nature and for its implications in terms of their own inner journey.

"The most significant contribution to an understanding of feminine psychology since Esther Harding's *Way of All Women*."—**Marion Woodman,** psychoanalyst and author of *The Owl Was a Baker's Daughter.*

Addiction to Perfection
The Still Unravished Bride

A Psychological Study by
Marion Woodman

12. Addiction to Perfection: The Still Unravished Bride.
Marion Woodman (Toronto). ISBN 0-919123-11-2. 208 pages. $12

"This book is about taking the head off an evil witch." With these words Marion Woodman begins her spiral journey, a powerful and authoritative look at the psychology and attitudes of modern woman.

The witch is a Medusa or a Lady Macbeth, an archetypal pattern functioning autonomously in women, petrifying their spirit and inhibiting their development as free and creatively receptive individuals. Much of this, according to the author, is due to a cultural one-sidedness that favors patriarchal values—productivity, goal orientation, intellectual excellence, spiritual perfection, etc.—at the expense of more earthy, interpersonal values that have traditionally been recognized as the heart of the feminine.

Marion Woodman's first book, *The Owl Was a Baker's Daughter: Obesity, Anorexia Nervosa and the Repressed Feminine,* focused on the psychology of eating disorders and weight disturbances.

Here, with a broader perspective on the same general themes, Marion Woodman continues her remarkable exploration of women's mysteries through case material, dreams, literature and mythology, in food rituals, rape symbolism, Christianity, imagery in the body, sexuality, creativity and relationships.

The final chapter, a discussion of the psychological meaning of ravishment (as opposed to rape), celebrates the integration of body and spirit and shows what this can mean to a woman in terms of her personal independence.

Studies in Jungian Psychology
by Jungian Analysts

LIMITED EDITION PAPERBACKS

Prices quoted are in U.S. dollars (except for Canadian orders)

1. The Secret Raven: Conflict and Transformation.
   Daryl Sharp (Toronto). ISBN 0-919123-00-7. 128 pages. $10

A concise introduction to the application of Jungian psychology. Focuses on the creative personality—and the life and dreams of the writer Franz Kafka —but the psychology is relevant to anyone who has experienced a conflict between the spiritual life and sex, or between inner and outer reality. (Knowledge of Kafka is not necessary.) Illustrated. Bibliography.

2. The Psychological Meaning of Redemption Motifs in Fairytales.
   Marie-Louise von Franz (Zurich). ISBN 0-919123-01-5. 128 pages. $10

A unique account of the significance of fairytales for an understanding of the process of individuation, especially in terms of integrating animal nature and human nature. Particularly helpful for its symbolic, nonlinear approach to the meaning of typical dream motifs (bathing, beating, clothes, animals, etc.), and its clear description of complexes and projection.

3. On Divination and Synchronicity: Psychology of Meaningful Chance.
   Marie-Louise von Franz (Zurich). ISBN 0-919123-02-3. 128 pages. $10

A penetrating study of the meaning of the irrational. Examines time, number, and methods of divining fate such as the I Ching, astrology, Tarot, palmistry, random patterns, etc. Explains Jung's ideas on archetypes, projection, psychic energy and synchronicity, contrasting Western scientific attitudes with those of the Chinese and so-called primitives. Illustrated.

4. The Owl Was a Baker's Daughter: Obesity, Anorexia Nervosa, and the Repressed Feminine.
   Marion Woodman (Toronto). ISBN 0-919123-03-1. 144 pages. $10

A pioneer work in feminine psychology, with particular attention to the body as mirror of the psyche in eating disorders and weight disturbances. Explores the personal and cultural loss—and potential rediscovery—of the feminine principle, through Jung's Association Experiment, case studies, dreams, Christianity and mythology. Illustrated. Glossary. Bibliography.

5. Alchemy: An Introduction to the Symbolism and the Psychology.
   Marie-Louise von Franz (Zurich). ISBN 0-919123-04-X. 288 pages. $16

A lucid and practical guide to what the alchemists were really looking for— emotional balance and wholeness. Completely demystifies the subject. An important work, invaluable for an understanding of images and motifs in modern dreams and drawings, and indispensable for anyone interested in relationships and communication between the sexes. 84 Illustrations.

6. Descent to the Goddess: A Way of Initiation for Women.
   Sylvia Brinton Perera (New York). ISBN 0-919123-05-8. 112 pages. $10

A timely and provocative study of women's freedom and the need for an inner, female authority in a masculine-oriented society. Based on the Sumerian goddess Inanna-Ishtar's journey to the underworld, her transformation through contact with her dark "sister" Ereshkigal, and her return. Rich in insights from dreams, mythology and analysis. Glossary. Bibliography.

7. **The Psyche as Sacrament: C.G. Jung and Paul Tillich.**
   John P. Dourley (Ottawa). ISBN 0-919123-06-6. 128 pages. $10

An illuminating, comparative study showing with great clarity that in the depths of the soul the psychological task and the religious task are one. With a dual perspective, the author—Jungian analyst and Catholic priest— examines the deeper meaning, for Christian and non-Christian alike, of God, Christ, the Spirit, the Trinity, morality and the religious life. Glossary.

8. **Border Crossings: Carlos Castaneda's Path of Knowledge.**
   Donald Lee Williams (Boulder). ISBN 0-919123-07-4. 160 pages. $12

The first thorough psychological examination of the popular don Juan novels. Using dreams, fairytales, and mythic and cultural parallels, the author brings Castaneda's spiritual journey down to earth, in terms of everyone's search for self-realization. Special attention to the psychology of women. (Familiarity with the novels is not necessary.) Glossary.

9. **Narcissism and Character Transformation: The Psychology of Narcissistic Character Disorders.**
   Nathan Schwartz-Salant (New York). ISBN 0-919123-08-2. 192 pp. $13

An incisive and comprehensive analysis of narcissism: what it looks like, what it means and how to deal with it. Shows how an understanding of the archetypal patterns that underlie the individual, clinical symptoms of narcissism can point the way to a healthy restructuring of the personality. Draws upon a variety of psychoanalytic points of view (Jungian, Freudian, Kohutian, Kleinian, etc.). Illustrated. Glossary. Bibliography.

10. **Rape and Ritual: A Psychological Study.**
    Bradley A. Te Paske (Minneapolis). ISBN 0-919123-09-0. 160 pp. $12

An absorbing combination of theory, clinical material, dreams and mythology, penetrating far beyond the actual deed to the impersonal, archetypal background of sexual assault. Special attention to male ambivalence toward women and the psychological significance of rape dreams and fantasies. Illustrated. Glossary. Bibliography.

11. **Alcoholism and Women: The Background and the Psychology.**
    Jan Bauer (Zurich). ISBN 0-919123-10-4. 144 pages. $12

A major contribution to an understanding of alcoholism, particularly in women. Compares and contrasts medical and psychological models, illustrates the relative merits of Alcoholics Anonymous and individual therapy, and presents new ways of looking at the problem based on case material, dreams and archetypal patterns. Glossary. Bibliography.

12. **Addiction to Perfection: The Still Unravished Bride.**
    Marion Woodman (Toronto). ISBN 0-919123-11-2. 208 pages. $12

A powerful and authoritative look at the psychology and attitudes of modern woman, expanding on the themes introduced in *The Owl Was a Baker's Daughter*. Explores the nature of the feminine through case material, dreams and mythology, in food rituals, rape symbolism, perfectionism, imagery in the body, sexuality and creativity. Illustrated.

13. **Jungian Dream Interpretation: A Handbook of Theory and Practice.**
    James A. Hall, M.D. (Dallas). ISBN 0-919123-12-0. 128 pages. $12

A comprehensive and practical guide to an understanding of dreams in light of the basic concepts of Jungian psychology. Jung's model of the psyche is described and discussed, with many clinical examples. Particular attention to common dream motifs, and how dreams are related to the stage of life and individuation process of the dreamer. Glossary.

14. The Creation of Consciousness: Jung's Myth for Modern Man.
Edward F. Edinger, M.D. (Los Angeles). ISBN 0-919123-13-9. 128 pp. $12
An important new book by the author of *Ego and Archetype,* proposing a world-view based on a creative collaboration between the scientific pursuit of knowledge and the religious search for meaning. Explores the significance of Jung's life and work, the meaning of human life and the pressing need for humanity to become conscious of its dark, destructive side. Illustrated.

15. The Analytic Encounter: Transference and Human Relationship.
Mario Jacoby (Zurich). ISBN 0-919123-14-7. 128 pp. $12
A sensitive study illustrating the difference between relationships based on projection and those characterized by psychological objectivity and mutual respect. Examines the views of Jung, Freud and Martin Buber, with special attention to the purpose of projection. Illustrated. Glossary. Bibliography.

16. Change of Life: Dreams and the Menopause.
Ann Mankowitz (Santa Fe). ISBN 0-919123-15-5. 128 pp. $12
A moving account of a menopausal woman's Jungian analysis, dramatically interweaving the experience of one woman with generally applicable social, biological, emotional and psychological factors. Frankly discusses the realities of aging, revealing the menopause as a time of rebirth, an opportunity for increased strength and specifically feminine wisdom. Bibliography.

17. The Illness That We Are: A Jungian Critique of Christianity.
John P. Dourley (Ottawa). ISBN 0-919123-16-3. 128 pp. $12
A radical study by Catholic priest and analyst, exploring the strengths and weaknesses of the Christian myth in terms of the psychological and religious search for wholeness. Special attention to Jung's views that the Gnostic, mystical and alchemical traditions contain the necessary compensation for the essentially extraverted and masculine ideals of Christianity.

18. Hags and Heroes: A Feminist Approach to Jungian Psychotherapy with Couples. ISBN 0-919123-17-1. 192 pp. $14
Polly Young-Eisendrath (Philadelphia)
A highly original contribution to couple therapy, integrating feminist views with the concepts of Jung and Harry Stack Sullivan. A wealth of helpful guidelines for both therapists and clients, including detailed suggestions for psychosexual and developmental assessment. Emphasis on revaluing the feminine and re-assessing the nature of female authority. Bibliography.

19. Cultural Attitudes in Psychological Perspective. 128 pp. $12
Joseph L. Henderson, M.D. (San Francisco). ISBN 0-919123-18-X.
A thoughtful new work by the author of *Thresholds of Initiation* and co-author of *Man and His Symbols.* Examines the nature and value of social, religious, aesthetic and philosophic attitudes, showing how the concepts of analytical psychology can give depth and substance to an individual *Weltanschauung* or world view. Illustrated. Bibliography.

Add $1 per book (bookpost) or $3 per book (airmail)

INNER CITY BOOKS
Box 1271, Station Q, Toronto, Canada M4T 2P4